How I Survived the First Five Years of Teaching

One Teacher's Journey

Sylvia A. Wright

WESTBOW
PRESS
A DIVISION OF THOMAS NELSON

WestBow Press books may be ordered through booksellers or by contacting:

WestBow Press
A Division of Thomas Nelson
1663 Liberty Drive
Bloomington, IN 47403
www.westbowpress.com
1-(866) 928-1240

ISBN: 978-1-4497-4967-5 (sc)
ISBN: 978-1-4497-4965-1 (hc)
ISBN: 978-1-4497-4966-8 (e)
Library of Congress Control Number: 2012907700

Printed in the United States of America

WestBow Press rev. date: 11/09/2012

To my family, especially Mom and Dad,
for always supporting me

Introduction

I remember looking through the career book in high school, trying to decide what I wanted to be when I grew up. I never considered being a teacher. I even commented that I would never be a teacher. I planned to major in business and establish my own magazine brand. I wasn't sure what type of magazine business I wanted to create, but I knew that was what I wanted to achieve one day.

However, things didn't work out that way.

After I accepted Jesus as my Lord and Savior and surrendered my life to Him, the desire to teach and to try to make a difference infiltrated my heart, and I realized that my purpose in life was to teach. From that day forward, I pursued my new goal of becoming a teacher. I began by recalling all of the teachers who made a difference in my life: Miss Beth Seavey, my sixth-grade science teacher; Mrs. Anne Rowe-Eddy, my eighth-grade language arts teacher; and Mrs. Karla Nembhard-Nicholas, my ninth-grade Spanish teacher. In my college years, the list continued to grow: Dr. Christine Hait, Dr. Ann Fleshman, and Dr. Melissa Heidari, who were my professors at Columbia College in South Carolina, and Ms. Beverly Miller, Dr. Brown, Dr. Charlotte Boger, and Dr. Virginia Dickens, my professors at Fayetteville State University in

North Carolina. These teachers influenced my life by mentoring me, helping me to improve my behavior, and helping me become a better writer, reader, and person.

During the last two years of my undergraduate studies at FSU, I had to do an enormous amount of research and write many papers about topics associated with education, especially teacher shortages and classroom management. I remember reading about the "revolving door" of teachers leaving the profession and the reasons they left. There were five reasons that seemed to be consistent in every article: lack of pay, lack of support from the administration, lack of student motivation, student misbehavior, and too much paperwork. I also remember reading several articles that said most new teachers leave the profession within the first five years, and if a teacher can survive the first five years of teaching, he or she is likely to stay in the profession.

I experienced most of these reasons for leaving the profession, and I almost left. However, I endured these challenges by learning how to cope with the situations, and I survived my first five years of teaching.

Chapter One

My First Teaching Experience

I graduated from Fayetteville State University in December 2003. Finding my first teaching position was difficult because the school year had already started. The process was also depressing.

My husband is in the Air Force, so we move frequently. We had recently moved from Fayetteville, North Carolina, to Sumter, South Carolina. I had a North Carolina teaching certificate, but I needed to apply for a South Carolina certificate in order to get a teaching job in South Carolina. I had heard that there was a teacher shortage in the state, so I thought that getting my certificate would be easy; all I had to do was fill out the application, apply for my South Carolina teacher's license, and easily land my first teaching position. Sadly, my assumptions were unrealistic.

I applied to several different counties—Sumter School District 17, Sumter School District 2 (Sumter was divided into two school districts), and Richland 1 School District in Columbia, which was about forty minutes away from Sumter. I was so desperate that I even called the principals at various schools, trying to land an interview. I thought that if I could just impress the principal, he or she might call down to the district office and request that I be assigned to his or her staff. However, every time I called, it was always the same question: "Do you have your South Carolina teaching certificate?"

I could not believe it. Positions were available, I had a bachelor's degree in middle grades English and a North Carolina teaching certificate, and I had passed all the required Praxis exams. What was the problem?

I called the South Carolina Department of Education Teacher Certification Office, and the customer service person told me that it could take them up to ninety days to process my application. Ninety days! I could not wait ninety days. I needed a job. I had one student loan that did not have a long grace period and other bills to pay which required more than one income. Once I graduated, I had to have a job.

When I realized that getting a job was not going to be as easy as I had thought, I became depressed. I thought our bills would start racking up, and we would have no way to pay them. How was I ever going to be able to work as a teacher?

One day, when I was picking my son up from school, I started talking to one of the school secretaries, Lucy Davis. I told her how I had just graduated from college and how I felt that I was getting the run-around from the Department of Education. With a smile, she handed me an application and said, "We need substitute teachers." (Lucy always found a positive side to everything.) I completed the application, and within a few weeks I had my first substitute teaching position—a two-day assignment for Ms. Hankins, a second-grade teacher. My son loved the fact that I was teaching at his school. He saw me in the hallway during his transitions to recess and lunch.

Ms. Hankins was a very organized teacher. She had a big schedule book on her desk that told me in detail what I was supposed to be doing each hour. Whenever I did not do something the way Ms. Hankins did it, the students let me know that I was not doing it correctly. For example, when I was reading a story the "wrong" way, they told me "Ms. Hankins reads the story this way, and she sits on her stool when she reads the story."

I liked substituting for Ms. Hankins, but when that assignment was over, I soon began to feel depressed again. I tried to have faith.

I knew the Lord was going to put me in the right place at the right time, but I wanted that time to be now.

It was February 2004, I still did not have a permanent teaching position, and the Department of Education had not processed my teaching certificate. I was very anxious. Why did it take so long? Did they not care that they were preventing me from getting a teaching position in South Carolina? Then one day I looked on the Sumter School District 17 website and saw that there was a teaching position advertised for the Academic Learning Center. I called the district office, and somehow I landed an interview with the assistant superintendent for human resources. I was excited!

Most of the interview went well. We discussed my student teaching and substitute teaching experience, and the assistant superintendent seemed please. Then the dreaded question came: "Do you have your South Carolina certificate?" I hated that question. I told him I had applied back in December and I still had not heard from the Department of Education. To my surprise he said, "That's okay."

Had I heard him correctly? He smiled at me and told me I would on the payroll as a long-term substitute. We shook hands, and I left. I was thrilled. I had really wanted to be on the payroll as a full-time, permanent teacher, but I could not afford to be choosy. This was clearly where I was supposed to be at this time.

After speaking with the assistant superintendent, I had another interview with Mr. Samuel Myers, the principal of the Academic Learning Center. On the day of the big interview with Mr. Myers, my spirits were high. I put on my best outfit and sprayed on my best perfume. I had already received the okay from the district office, so the only obstacle left was my meeting with the principal.

In order to get this job, I would have to impress him and show him that I was serious about this position, which I was.

The interview was wonderful. After he started talking to me like I already worked there, I knew he liked me and wanted me on his staff. He took me on a tour of the school and said, "This will be your classroom." Wow! My very own classroom! He told me that I would be teaching middle school language arts (English and reading) and high school English. I had a lot of preps, but I did not care—I was that desperate. After the tour, he asked me if I could start the next day, and I calmly told him I could. I wanted to yell it, but I controlled myself.

The next day I arrived at the Academic Learning Center early, just as happy and thankful as could be. I finally had a job. I may not have been considered a teacher on the books, but I knew I had the credentials and I knew I was a teacher.

The first thing I did when I went into my classroom was look for ways to decorate it since the walls were too bare. I did not have any posters or anything special to put on the walls, so I found little things that the previous teacher had left and put them up. I organized the materials that were given to me, and the bell rang.

The morning started with everybody—teachers and students—meeting in a large, spacious room across the hallway from my classroom. I entered the room through the side door, nervous because I was minutes away from standing in front of the students in my classroom all alone. Having your own classroom is different from student teaching or substitute teaching because that's someone else's classroom. During my student teaching experience, my lead teacher left me by myself at one point to teach the class, but it was still *her* classroom and *her* students.

After all the students and teachers were gathered in this room, Mr. Myers read the morning announcements. Guess who was a part of the announcements! I should have known that he was going to introduce me since I was new to the school, but my focus was on being alone and in front of students for the first time. Mr. Myers said, "I would like for you all to welcome Mrs. Wright. She is our new English teacher."

I remember feeling all the eyes in the room on me and sweating profusely. (I think I changed deodorant after that day because it was no longer strong enough.) After the announcements, the students were dismissed to their classes.

When I went back to my classroom, I met Ms. Johnson, the teacher's assistant. She showed me where the previous teacher had kept the files and where the teaching materials were located. I taught sixth and seventh grade before lunch, and the eighth graders and high school students after lunch. One of my biggest challenges that year was trying to find assignments that would accommodate each high school grade since I had students that were in four different grades.

Later that day, Ms. Johnson told me about the previous teacher, who had quit because she could not deal with the students' behavior. I also learned that I was teaching at an alternative school, a school for students who did not know how to behave in a regular school setting. Mr. Myers might have mentioned the type of school setting in our interview, but the only thing I was listening for was "Yes, you have the job."

After I came to know my students, I learned that some of them knew that their behavior had been wrong and had vowed to change their ways once they returned to their regular school. Others did not care about regular school and liked being in the alternative setting since the school and the classes were smaller and they had more one-on-one opportunities with the teacher. A few of the students needed something more than what an alternative setting could offer them; some of my students had been to the juvenile detention center several times, and they acted like they were not afraid of anything. Some teachers might have been intimidated in this type of teaching situation, but I did not see students who had been kicked out of their regular schools because they were bad; I saw regular students who needed someone to teach them what they needed to know so they could graduate from high school. They knew that was how I felt, and they respected me for the way I respected them.

A few days into my new teaching job, my teacher friend, Kelly, gave me some more posters and teaching materials that she had from when she taught elementary school language arts, before she changed to middle school math. She helped me form a system for my grades and showed me how to print forms to keep up with my attendance. Kelly was a life-saver; I did not have a mentor or an experienced teacher to show me what to do. I was only shown my classroom, the books I was supposed to use to teach the class, and where to go if I wanted to look at a student's file. I was not given a book to record grades or attendance.

I also did not have a curriculum guide that showed me what I should be teaching, so I had to develop my own lesson plans for each class day by day. I decided to print the South Carolina English/language arts teaching standards for each grade level and develop lessons using those standards. I remember starting my job on a Thursday, which was great because I had the students do an autobiography project about their lives the first two days while I created my teaching curriculum. It was an enormous amount of work. Thinking back on it, I put in a ridiculous amount of hours for someone who was receiving only substitute pay. However, I was a teacher. I might not have been paid like a teacher, but I was going to make sure I was the best one I could be.

Weeks went by, and I finally got the hang of teaching. I had my lessons planned, which I had to turn into Mr. Myers each week; I had a grading system going; and I was keeping track of attendance.

Then it happened. I experienced the first and so far the only fight between students in my classroom.

We were working on how to write paragraphs, so I took my seventh-grade students outside and told them that the theme of their paragraph was nature. They could choose any subject they saw while we were outside, as long as it was about nature. After thirty minutes, we went back into the classroom and I asked for volunteers to share their paragraph. One student stood up and read a wonderful paragraph about ants and how they work together as a family. After she finished reading her paragraph, she sat back down, and the girl who sat behind her told her that her paragraph was stupid.

As if everyone knew what was going to happen next, the mood of the entire class changed. The two girls had been friends, but something had happened between them outside of school, so now they were enemies. The girl who had read her paragraph stood up, the other girl stood up to face her, and neither one of them would back down.

I stood between them and asked them not to fight because they were good students, and if they fought there would be serious consequences for both of them—they could even be kicked out of the program. I pleaded with the girl who had read her paragraph because she was one of the students who had vowed to change her ways and never end up in this program again, but she looked at me straight in the eyes and said in a quiet voice, "Mrs. Wright, please move. I don't want you to get hurt. She should not have said that about me."

Before I could get out the way, the other student pulled the hair of the girl I was pleading with and fists started flying. Ms. Johnson was already at the door calling for help—unlike me, who was trying to be a negotiator. Ms. Johnson and I yelled for someone to come and break up the fight because we weren't going to be able to do it. Finally, after at least three minutes of these girls knocking the juice out of each other, help arrived. The girls were separated, sent to the office, and suspended for a few days. I was glad that they were allowed to stay in the program because they were both good students; they just needed to deal with the other conflict they had had outside of school and didn't know any other way to do it.

One of my fondest memories at ALC was when I taught *Romeo and Juliet*, my favorite of Shakespeare's plays, to the high school class. I assigned characters, and the students read their assigned parts while I stopped them periodically to explain the scene in their terms: Mercutio and Romeo were homeboys, Romeo was on the rebound because Rosalind dumped him, Mercutio convinced him to go to the party at Capulet's house to meet girls and take his mind off Rosalind, and so on.

The best part was seeing their final projects. They were allowed to get into small groups and choose between writing and performing a rap or song about the play, or writing an ABC book using words or ideas from the play. (I know the latter project sounds easy, but I wanted everyone to participate, and if the requirements were too hard, I'd run the risk of a small number of students participating and the others not turning in their assignments.)

The boys liked the idea of a rap, and the girls tended to stick with the ABC book. One of the boys' groups created a phenomenal rap, and the brother of one of the students owned equipment that allowed the group to mix beats and record their rap on a CD. In fact, all of the assignments were great, and I was very proud of all the groups for being so creative. They were so impressed with themselves that they asked Mr. Myers to visit the classroom so they could show him what they had learned. He was impressed!

I finally received my South Carolina teaching certificate in May, which was much longer than ninety days. While I had been able to earn an income, having my certificate opened up more doors for me because I was now considered a "highly qualified" teacher and could now formally be called a "teacher." I spoke with Mr. Myers about changing my title at the district office, but I ran into another brick wall. I was told that, since it was so late in the school year, I would have to stay listed as a long-term substitute and that my status would be updated to teacher the next school term.

I was irritated with the process. I had known all along that I was a certified teacher—I was just waiting on this piece of paper—so why couldn't my status be updated now? I felt that I had already been cheated out of my due pay for all this time; now they want me to continue to receive substitute pay even though I was fully certified.

I told Kelly what was going on, and she told me I should work at her school in August. Wow! How cool that would be to work with my friend! I looked at her with eyes full of joy and asked her what I needed to do to get the job. She told me I had to fill out an application at the Sumter School District 2 human resources office and be interviewed. I knew that would be easy because I already had an application on file from when I applied to all the school districts in and around Sumter. All I needed was an interview, and I did not have any problem getting one.

"So why do you want to be a teacher?" asked Mr. James Wilson, the human resources administrator. I answered from the heart and added some of what I had written about my educational philosophy. Then he asked me why I wanted to teach at Mayewood Middle School. I told him the truth: "Because my friend Kelly works there." As it turned out, he had hired Kelly, so he knew exactly whom I was talking about. Kelly had a great reputation with the district, so he considered her a great reference. He asked me a few more questions, and by the end of the interview, I was the new sixth grade language arts teacher at Mayewood Middle School for the 2004-2005 school year.

The only problem was how to tell Mr. Myers, the man who had given me my first job when I was down in the dumps. After school the next day, I went to Mr. Myers' office. I knocked on his door and he waved me into his office. I told him as gently as I could that I did not plan on returning to the Academic Learning Center because I would be working at Mayewood Middle School as a sixth-grade language arts teacher. He was quiet at first, and then he looked me square in the eye and said, "Whatever makes you happy. I have never been the type of person to hold a teacher back."

I was relieved. He was not mad at all, even though I felt as though I had betrayed him. As I was leaving, he asked me why I chose to go to Mayewood, and I told him that I had a friend who worked there, and I preferred teaching one grade level instead of several. When he commented that Mayewood was a very challenging place, I wondered what could be more challenging than the Academic Learning Center?

While the conversation ended on a positive note, I think he was a little upset that I was leaving, but he was not mad at me. During the next week, the staff learned about my plans to teach at Mayewood, and various people told me that the kids were bad and that it would be a challenging school. I had thought that the Academic Learning Center was supposed to be a "bad" and "challenging" place; after all, it was an alternative school. I could not believe they were telling me that this regular school was going to worse than an alternative school.

June could not arrive fast enough for me. When summer break was finally at hand, I had worked for only four months and I was burnt out. People who say teachers don't need a break need to try being a teacher for a few days, and I guarantee they'll re-evaluate their viewpoint. It was a bittersweet goodbye, as the Academic Learning Center had been my first real teaching experience. I was sad, but I was also happy that I would no longer have to plan for so many classes and that I would be seen as a full-fledged, qualified teacher at my new school.

Chapter Two

Finally a Teacher

Teachers had to report to their assigned schools during the third week of August, and I could hardly wait to get to Mayewood and set up my classroom. I did not have many posters or decorations for my room, but what I did have, I hot-glued to the sea-green cinderblock wall. One of the differences between Mayewood and the Academic Learning Center was the presence of teams. There were three teams at Mayewood: the sixth-grade team, the seventh-grade team, and the eighth-grade team. Of course, I was on the sixth-grade team. Rhonda, who taught social studies, was the sixth-grade team leader, while Margaret taught science, and Leroy taught math.

During the first few teacher workdays, I was in meeting after meeting. I barely had time to do anything in my classroom, so I went in early each day to do little things like set up my grade book and attendance roster in the Filemaker Pro grade book system. With this electronic grade book, all I had to do was type in my students' names and I could create a grade book and an attendance roster for each class. My grades were automatically calculated for me, and I could print out progress reports.

During the in-service week, I received a curriculum guide that listed teacher activities, student activities, and assessments that were supposed to be used during each unit. After having to plan out my own curriculum at the Academic Learning Center, I thought having it all done for me would be great, but this was brutal. I did not like how everything was scripted out. I felt that my creativity was tossed out the window and that the lessons were not genuine. They were lessons that other teachers created and I was supposed to do it the way they wrote it.

For almost a week, I had been in training after training, and during the little time that was left, I prepared for the first day of school. August 19, 2004, the first day of school, arrived early, and so did I. I signed in at the office, checked my mailbox, and walked to my classroom. I rehearsed in my head how the day was going to go. Then *"ring!"* and in came my first-period class. I was nervous as I looked at all the little faces staring at me, on center stage. I introduced myself and told them basic information about myself, and they shared something about themselves. I told them the rules, and *"ring!"* it was time for second period. The day rushed by, and each class was the same thing: introductions and then the rules.

At lunchtime, I went to Kelly's classroom and she asked how everything was going. I told her I was no longer nervous, but I felt like a robot repeating myself each class period. By the end of the last period of the day, I was exhausted. I picked up my children, Perry and Karla, from school, made dinner (to be honest, I might have stopped for chicken nuggets that night), and went straight to bed. I had never been so tired in my life.

The next day I issued books and started into my scripted curriculum. That day went by fast too, and I was just as exhausted when it ended as I had been the day before. I was glad that school had started in the middle of the week because I needed that weekend to relax and stop my head from spinning.

Monday morning came, and I was back into the routine: arrive early, sign in, check my mailbox, first period bell, teach. After school, I had to attend a new teacher's induction class that would be held every other Monday for three hours after school during my first year of teaching. We would meet in a conference room in the district office where we learned strategies to prevent us from becoming stressed out, how to talk to parents during a parent conference, and when it was appropriate call parents about a misbehaving student. "Remember to say something positive first," said Sharon Delaney, the coordinator of the class. She always offered good advice.

In one of the first sessions, we received a big packet that was an example of a veteran teacher's STEP notebook. It had a course syllabus, a list of materials and resources the teacher planned to use during the year, pages explaining how the teacher planned to contact parents, and classroom routines. (There were so many pages of different things required for this notebook that it should have been called the ETP, Enormous Teacher Portfolio.) We were expected to construct our own STEP notebook. I felt like I was taking another college course: I had to gather and write about all this information, which filled a three-ringed binder, and turn it in to my assistant principal. I was starting to feel overwhelmed.

The session I thought was most beneficial was the one in which we discussed the curriculum guide. This was a sensitive topic for me because I hated how everything was prescribed for me. A curriculum guide would have been great when I was at the Academic Learning Center because I had been writing my own lesson plans for four different grade levels. Now I felt like I had to conform to these scripted assignments that worked for another teacher. How did they know whether they would work for me in my classroom? I was thankful for the discussion we had that night because someone clarified that the assignments and activities were only suggestions; it was okay for me to change the activities and assignments to fit the needs of my classroom, as long as I used the assigned short stories and poems that were listed in the guide and structured my assignments or activities using the SC benchmark standards listed for that week. Therefore, my perception of the curriculum guide had been completely wrong; I still could use my creativity in my lessons.

Later in the year, the meetings turned into therapy sessions, as everybody was dealing with some type of drama with the principal, another teacher, a student or students, or a parent.

At the beginning of the year, I set up routines with all my classes. When the students came in to class, they had ten minutes to complete a journal assignment that was written on the board. I used this strategy so the students had something to do right away and would not be tempted to engage in off-task behavior. I used a timer to help me keep track of the time. I also established the rules, consequences, and rewards at the beginning of the year. Mayewood had an intervention program for which teachers had to fill out a form entitled "MMS Intervention Logs." The form had three boxes in which teachers were to document three incidents and the types of interventions used with the student before we were allowed to refer students to the office. This approach aligned perfectly with my theories about establishing consequences. After I gave a student a warning, the first intervention was isolation/ time out from the group and a conference with the student. The second intervention was lunch detention and parent contact. The third intervention was a parent conference either by phone or face to face.

While the students were aware of the rules and these interventions, unfortunately, most of them did not care. During the first few weeks, everything went as expected; however, I soon realized that I had started out being too nice, and some of the students began to take me for a joke because my tone was too friendly. I was not authoritative enough. I had minor behavior management problems in a few of my classes, but nothing compared to what went on in my fourth-period class. I had so many issues with that class that I learned my lesson, and after that year I never started a year using a friendly tone. I wasn't mean, I was just firm.

I hated fourth period. It was my largest class and my worst class. It seemed as if all the kids with behavior problems were placed together. (Instead of students being mixed up each class period, they were grouped together and went to all their classes together.) Each sixth-grade teacher had a share of this class, but they were with me during the longest period of the day. I taught for thirty minutes and then stopped and took them to lunch, after which we returned to class to continue where we left off. This was hard because the students had a difficult time settling down after lunch, especially since they had no free time outside. (The extra time that had once been allotted for recess was added to fourth period as extra academic time.) During this extra academic period, I taught mini-lessons from a PACT workbook, which was used to prepare students for the Palmetto Achievement Challenge Test, the South Carolina standardized test, and the students had to answer practice questions. The students did not take this time seriously, and I dreaded the thought of having to teach that period every day. I wanted third period to last forever!

My feelings did not start out that way, but it was only a few weeks into the school year when I started filling out intervention logs, day after day, student after student. It seemed as if all my energy was being exhausted disciplining students for disrespectful and disruptive behavior. I would be in the front of class teaching a lesson, and students would start talking to each other as if I were not even there. One girl threw things in class—paper, pen parts, and anything else she felt like throwing. I filled out her intervention log. Another student tapped on his desk, making all kinds of noises even after I asked him several times to stop. He did not care, and I filled out his intervention log. Students talked back to me and refused to listen to me. I filled out their intervention logs. If there had been an award for the class with the most intervention logs, it would have been my fourth period.

I followed the rules: I gave the students three interventions before I wrote the referrals. Once I had the documentation that was required to write a referral to the office, I wrote the referral, attached the white copy of the intervention log to the referral, and kept the yellow copy. I turned them into the assistant principal, who was in charge of discipline. When I checked my mailbox the next day, I found copies of the referrals with "conferenced with student and parent contacted" written at the bottom. That was it. I was dismayed by the lack of discipline. These students were refusing to listen to me. I had had a conference with them, they had served lunch detention—which meant I had to sit by them during lunch—and I had called and spoken with their parents, and the only punishment they got the next time they misbehaved was more of the same.

After I overcame my feelings of disappointment, I thought that maybe the assistant principal would take some further action the next time she received a referral on a student with whom she had already "conferenced with," so I continued to follow the procedure of the intervention logs. However, I soon realized that the only time a student was punished in any meaningful way was if he or she struck the principal or brought a weapon to school. Nothing else was punished. It was like a bad behavior free-for-all, and the students loved it.

After the other students realized that nothing was going to happen to them for disrespecting me, more students joined the bandwagon. I had a small group—maybe four out of the twenty-four kids—who wanted to learn, but they couldn't because the other students in their class realized that my class could be turned into a zoo, and the administrators did not care. I felt sorry for these four, and I wished that they could have been reassigned to another group of students, but I had no administrative power—and no support from the administration in dealing with students who threatened to take over my class.

I had to take matters into my own hands.

I decided to write a word on the board, such as "recess," and every time the class misbehaved, I erased a letter. If the class made it through the week with at least one letter still on the board, they earned a reward. It worked for a while, and they earned a reward once or twice, but soon this incentive lost its power.

Next I tried working on individual behaviors. I pulled out the classroom management notebook I had created in Dr. Kosterman's class. One type of student that immediately stood out was "The Influencer." The Influencer in my fourth-period class was older than the other students because she had failed a previous grade. If she didn't do work, they didn't do work. If she was rude, they were rude. Checking my classroom management guide, I identified her need: power. She did not see her mother often because her mother was always working, so she was almost always on her own, and she was used to being in charge of everything. To fulfill her need for power I put her in charge of a literature circle group, and I allowed her to pass out papers and collect things. I had a private talk with her and told her how smart she was and that her behavior was affecting her grade, and she and I eventually formed a relationship. For the most part, she listened when I asked her to do something, but not all the time. The class would run smoothly when she was submissive or absent, but she was rarely absent.

I called the parents of the students who had been disruptive and uncooperative and asked them to come to the class and sit with their children. Only three parents came. One parent became infuriated by the lack of respect she observed and lectured the students about the importance of education and how they were only hurting themselves. She then turned to her son and gave him a strict warning that if I ever called the house about his behavior again, he would regret it. She couldn't bear to stay the entire period, so she went to the principal and complained about the lack of respect the students were exhibiting toward me, even with a parent in the classroom, and she questioned what the administration was doing to help me discipline this class. The answer was: not much.

While another parent was visiting, one of my problem students, decided to be more disruptive than usual by tapping on her desk with her pencil and humming while I was teaching. I knew that neither the assistant principal nor the principal would do anything about her behavior so I tried to ignore it and move on. Since I didn't want to give her attention, I walked to her desk and gently took the pencil, but then she banged on her desk with her hand. The more I ignored her, the more annoying she became. I was embarrassed, knowing that there was a parent sitting in the back of my classroom watching as this situation unfolded, but the parent just shook his head as he looked at the student.

Finally, I told the student that she was not only disrespecting me but her classmates, and she was hurting herself and them by preventing everyone from learning. I guess she didn't like my calling her out—which bewildered me because her goal was to get attention—as she yelled that she was going to see the assistant principal and as she left my classroom, she charged toward me, deliberately ramming one side of her body into my shoulder.

My reflexes took control. I extended my arm and pushed her away from me. Then she became even more belligerent, screaming and kicking the walls outside of my classroom. As a result of one of her kicks, there was a black scuff mark on my door. She was so loud and unruly that the other teachers looked out of their classrooms, but when they saw who the student was, they went back into their classes. After she kicked another wall and screamed a little more, she headed towards the assistant principal's office. I wanted the parents to see what type of behavior I dealt with daily, but this situation surpassed the usual disrespectful and disruptive behavior.

I was shocked that the assistant principal didn't ask me about the incident because this was her favorite student. I went to the assistant principal and told her what had happened, and she said that the student had already told her. I told her my side of the story and was baffled by her dismissal of the situation. She really didn't seem to care what I had to say. Nothing happened to the student, and she started reporting to the assistant principal's office during my class. The other students complained that it was not fair that this student was receiving special treatment for misbehaving. I was surprised that they were upset that she wasn't punished for how she had behaved, and some of the students even went to the assistant principal and expressed their feelings about the situation.

Eventually the student began coming to my class again. The assistant principal had created a monster and she knew it. On several occasions, the student walked out of my class without permission and went to the assistant principal's office, and the assistant principal walked her back to my class and, in a casual tone, told her not to leave the class. Of course, she didn't listen. Once the student walked out of my room when the assistant principal was in a meeting, and she became upset because the assistant principal was unable to meet with her at that moment. Instead of returning to my class, she went to the main office and waited for the assistant principal. The assistant principal again expressed to the student—this time in a more "serious" tone—that she could not walk out of class whenever she felt like it, and she could not use the assistant principal's open-door privilege to skip my class. This made the girl mad because she felt that she was being betrayed since she viewed the assistant principal more as a friend than an authority figure. (She was not the only student who had this view.)

The students' perception of the assistant principal was detrimental to teachers, and it affected the students' behavior in class. They knew that if they disrespected the teacher or misbehaved in class, there would be no real consequence because the assistant principal, their buddy, would work it out with the teacher. I remember telling one of my students that I would send him to the principal's office if he continued to misbehave, and he happily responded that he didn't care and begged me to do so. Since the students' perception of the assistant principal and the principal as disciplinary figures was a joke, most of the teachers refused to send students to the office. Going to the office had become a reward.

The word spread among the parents about the behavior I was dealing with in my fourth-period class, and some of the parents wanted their kids moved out of the class with the "bad" kids. The irony was that some of parents who demanded their children be moved were actually the parents of the kids who were contributing to the problem! That idea never developed into anything, and the students who wanted to learn had to stay in a class with students who did not.

I was not the only teacher who had such issues, and my referrals were not the only ones with "conferenced with student and parent contacted" written at the bottom. We were all dealing with rude and disrespectful behavior in our classrooms, and students rarely received any type of disciplinary action. The students were out of control. It seemed like the administration thought the problem laid in our classroom management because that was the focus of several staff meetings. We watched a video that featured two teachers modeling their classroom management techniques. The students sat obediently in their seats, showed respect to their teacher, and raised their hands to answer questions, and the teachers talked softly. I was not the only teacher in the school who was offended by this video. We felt that this video was not an accurate example of our population of kids. Some students in our classes did not listen to their parents or the administration and did not care about consequences. Show me a video that teaches me how to deal with these types of students, and I will pay attention. I want to see a teacher model what she does when a student continues to tap on his desk and make noises, despite warnings to stop. What interventions does she use? We did not have perfect teaching situations, so why were they showing us a video about teachers who did?

We decided that we would take care of our own discipline.

As a team, we met in Rhonda's room at least once a week and discussed issues that involved the sixth grade. We all had similar problems with the same students and received no support from the administration, so we brainstormed ideas as a team to combat the situation. One of the first interventions we tried was team lunch detention. We had to eat lunch with our students, as there were no assistants to watch the kids during lunch. We designated an area for students who had misbehaved, and they had to eat their lunches quietly, away from their friends. However, the students eventually turned lunch detention into a game. Since students had to sit with their fourth-period class at lunch, groups of friends would try to get detention together so they could sit near their friends from different classes. We would separate them by putting them into corners throughout the lunchroom if they were caught talking to one another, but we could never enjoy our lunches because we were busy trying to catch violators.

Then we decided to give the students free time on Fridays, and if a student misbehaved during the week, he or she had to stand against the wall the entire time. This strategy worked better than lunch detention because the boys wanted to play football, and the girls loved to sit on the bleachers and talk with their friends. Another intervention we tried was Think Time, a strategy that the seventh-grade team was using to deal with their problem students. (Since no one except a select few teachers who had worked with the principal at a previous school were receiving administrative support, we teachers bounced ideas off each other and tried to find strategies that worked.) A misbehaving student who was given Think Time was sent to another teacher's classroom to write down how they were misbehaving and give examples of the proper way to behave in class. If the student felt that he or she could exhibit the proper behavior, he or she was allowed to return to class. We each knew which students we could tolerate, so we decided which teacher the student would to go to when we used this strategy. I know you're wondering whether this would disrupt the other teacher's class, and sometimes it did, but that's an example of how we all worked together. We bore each other's burdens.

Eventually the principal came to my class to give the students a "serious" talking-to, but before she could finish, one of the girls started talking. When the principal asked her to be quiet, the student rolled her eyes and said, "Whatever." The principal told her to go to her office and quickly ended her speech. She instantly gave that student a day of in-school suspension, which I found appalling since I'd had to tolerate this type of behavior every day and the students I referred, after I painstakingly filled out my intervention logs, never got more than a slap on the wrist. Toward the end of the year, the assistant principal and the principal started to assign more students to ISS and suspend them for their misbehavior, but it was too late. The students really did not care what punishment was given to them.

I learned to cope with the students who were misbehaving by focusing on the students who were trying to learn, and I learned to choose my battles. I was told later that the assistant principal had not disciplined my students because she thought that the problem was my classroom management, not my students. I couldn't believe it. How was I expected to manage my class when I did not have support from the administration? I was essentially a first-year teacher, and I needed support from the administration and parents.

What had I gotten myself into? This school needed Joe Clark! The warnings from my previous colleagues at the Academic

Learning Center had been true: Mayewood was more challenging than an alternative school. I could not believe that a "regular" school was worse than a school full of kids who had been kicked out of regular schools. I talked to Kelly many times during the year about my fourth-period class because she lived only one house away from me on Shaw Air Force Base. I was at her house many times, and we talked for hours about the things that happened at Mayewood. She did not have a class from Hades as I did, but she had problem students that she was dealing with, so we vented to each other. One of the best things about working at Mayewood with Kelly was being able to go to her classroom when I was having a bad day; seeing her during the day reminded me of being back at home on the base.

Kelly wasn't the only person who helped me survive during my first full year of teaching. I loved my team. Rhonda and Margaret were veteran teachers at Mayewood, so they had taught many of the students' brothers and sisters. I think some of the kids treated Rhonda and Margaret differently because they had taught their brothers and sisters, but Leroy and I were fresh teacher meat. It was Leroy's second year and my first. My fourth-period class was his fifth-period class, and after they left me, they went across the hall to him. He tried to act like they did not act up in his class, but we knew they did. We could hear him fussing at them.

Our weekly team meetings were therapy sessions, and Rhonda's room was next to mine, so if I ever needed to talk to someone immediately about a problem, I walked next door. She always used southern idioms to make me feel better and always knew how to make me laugh. For example, she lived near Mayewood, so when she needed to go to the grocery store, she would say she had to go to "town" which was about ten or fifteen minutes away. Whenever she said this in her southern accent, it reminded me of the times I went to visit my grandma in Alabama, where the nearest "town" was Tuskegee, fifteen or twenty minutes away. It might not seem funny, but hearing Rhonda say "town" cracked me up every time. She knew it too, so if I was sad or having a bad day, she always said, "I have to go to town today," and we started laughing. I could call her today, and if she just said the word "town," it would still make me chuckle.

June finally arrived. This year was filled with trials and tribulations, but I survived my first year of teaching, and I no longer had to see that hellish fourth-period class again! Thank God for summer vacation!

Chapter Three

Back at Mayewood

W here do I start in describing this complex, eventful year? This was the year that the school was visited by the External Review Team, I had an evaluation nightmare, and there were new teachers from India who had no support. At least the students were better—for the most part.

It was the third week in August 2005, and teachers had to report to their assigned schools. During my first year, I had to go to many different trainings, seminars, and teacher conferences around South Carolina, so I traveled to Florence, Columbia, and Myrtle Beach. My favorite teacher conference was in Myrtle Beach, as I took away ideas about improving student vocabulary, designating a reading area in my classroom to promote reading, building my classroom library, and adding color to my classroom to make students feel welcome. Teachers were given $250 every year, with which they had to buy their own school supplies for the entire year, and I used mine to improve my classroom. I purchased a rug decorated with books, two beach chairs, a mushroom chair, a night stand, three mini-bookstands to place on top of the nightstand because I planned to showcase three books each month, an enormous number of books from Scholastic that accommodated all reading levels from picture books to high-level novels, magazines for the reluctant readers, and fabrics to use on my bulletin board. I have to credit Mrs. Schrader for giving me the fabric idea; I have never used bulletin board paper again, as the fabric is more colorful and durable than paper.

I was so proud of myself. I knew that this year was going to be better. I had a lovely welcome bulletin board outside of my classroom and colorful bulletin boards inside my classroom. I had a designated reading area with a rug and chairs and books for students to read. I was even given a big bookshelf, which was made from cherry wood, where I separated my books by genre. Kelly helped me out by giving me tons of books that I could keep because she wouldn't need them any longer since she was sticking with math.

During this school year, I worked on my master's degree in the Divergent Learning program at Columbia College in Columbia, South Carolina. Every weekend during the fall and spring semesters I spent two nights in Columbia. I attended one class Friday evening, two classes on Saturday, and one class on Sunday afternoon. After my Saturday classes, I did the required research for my thesis and the work for my other classes. I was tired on Fridays after teaching all day then attending class in the evening, but it was all worth it.

The Divergent Learning program was perfect for me because I learned strategies I could use to help students who did not perform well in a traditional classroom environment. By "traditional classroom environment," I mean teacher-led discussions in a classroom in which the desks are always in straight rows and students work alone, rarely doing group work. For my thesis, I researched the difference between traditional teacher-directed learning and cooperative learning and concluded that it was best to have a balance between the two teaching styles.

During this year, I implemented more cooperative learning opportunities in my classes. In some classes, things went smoothly, but in others, the students goofed off and did not follow the directions. One student could not work with anyone; no matter which group I put him in, there was always conflict, and he ended up working by himself on some occasions. Overall, the students enjoyed working in groups, and some groups had good discussions.

I had learned about the kinds of intelligences and types of learners during my undergraduate years, but that information took on new meaning now that I'd had some experience, and I was able to use my experience in one of my master's classes. Knowing the curriculum from the year before was also beneficial because I knew what I was required to teach, so I revised my lesson plans to incorporate ways to accommodate the different types of learners in my class. For example, part of the curriculum was to read the short story, "Tuesday of the Other June," which was about a nice girl named June who was bullied by a mean girl who was also named June. The year before, we did the vocabulary activities, wrote a summary of the story, discussed the plot, completed the discussion questions, and had a brief conversation about bullying and how it affects people. This year, in addition to what we did last year, we watched clips from the movie *Hope Floats*, when Bernice was bullied by Big Dolores. The clips were similar to the conflict between June and the mean June, but the outcomes were different. I drew a huge diagram on bulletin board paper, and we compared and contrasted the bullies and the victims. Students broke into groups to discuss the similarities and differences, and then students from each group took turns writing something in the class Venn diagram. The students were active and engaged, they enjoyed seeing the movie clips, and the lesson accommodated auditory, visual, and kinesthetic learners. I did not make every lesson like that, but I was more cognizant of the importance of engaging all learners when I planned my lessons. I also discovered PowerPoint that year, so I revised some of my lessons to integrate PowerPoint presentations.

During the in-service week, which was held at the beginning of the school year, I came early to school each day so I could set up my classroom. I knew that, like the previous year, we would have little time in our classrooms for that task, as we would spend the majority of the week in meetings and trainings. I was one of the first teachers to have my room set up and ready to go, and all I had left to do was to look over my lesson plans and determine what I would teach differently. I thought I would use the time the other teachers were using to set up their rooms to work on my lesson plans, but I was mistaken.

Mr. Omprakash Mekala, Mrs. Sri Devi Dasyam, and Mrs. Mumtaz Shaik were new teachers at Mayewood, but they were not new to the teaching profession. Mr. Mekala, the new sixth-grade math teacher, had a master's degree in math and had been a math teacher in India for twenty years. Mrs. Shaik, the new eighth-grade English teacher, had been an elementary teacher in India for five years. Mrs. Dasyam, the new seventh-grade math teacher, had a master's degree in math and education, had been a university professor in India, and had been teaching for thirteen years.

Mrs. Dasyam and I instantly connected. One day, after we were dismissed from one of our trainings, she walked with me to my classroom, where she saw all of the posters I had around the room, the colorful bulletin boards, and the reading area. She was so impressed that she told Mr. Mekala and Mrs. Shaik, who wanted to know how they could get posters and other items for their bulletin boards. I told them about the teacher supply store off of S. Pike West and Wal-Mart off of Broad Street. Just as I was about to start on my lesson plans, they shared with me that they did not do all this decorating in India and that they had no transportation to get to the stores. I felt sorry for them; here they were, in an unknown environment, in a new culture, with no transportation—they were dropped off at the school in the morning and picked up after school. Mayewood was a little school in the country, and the teacher store and Walmart were not right around the corner. (We had to go to "town" for these things.) I decided that I would work on my lesson plans that weekend and took these three new teachers to the teacher store for posters and other supplies. Then we went to Walmart and they purchased fabric for their bulletin boards, and glue guns along with glue sticks for their posters. (We couldn't use staples or tape to put things on the wall since our classroom walls were cinderblock.)

The next day, after the training, I went to each one of their rooms and helped them put up their posters and create their bulletin boards. By the end of the week, their classrooms were ready to go. They were very grateful, and I was glad to do it, as there was no representative from the district office to make sure these teachers had what they needed. These professionals might not have been new teachers, but they were new to America and American customs. I may have given up the time to revise my lesson plans, but I was able to help other teachers, and that made me feel good.

August 18, 2005, was the first day of school. In each of my classes, I established the rules and routines for the year, I shared something about myself, and the students shared things about themselves. Before I knew it, it was the end of the day. This year was going to be better than the last year had been. When students came into the room, they had ten minutes to do the warm-up assignment that was on the board, after which they could read silently. One of the skills I wanted to focus on was increasing student vocabulary, so I gave the students two analogies each day for their warm-up instead of journal writing.

The reading area was a hit. Some students would race to finish their warm-up assignment so they could read in the mushroom chair. I also had the siblings of some of the students from last year, and I sensed that I had some teacher points for teaching their brothers and sisters. One of my former students came into my classroom one day and told me that she had told her sister that I was her favorite teacher and not to act up in my class. It was funny because whenever this student acted up in class, I mentioned her sister and she would say, "All right, Mrs. Wright. Dang!"

The students this year also cared when I threatened to call their parents. The previous year, when I told certain students that I was going to call their parents, they offered me the cell phone number. I enjoyed all of my classes, and there was no class from Hades, but I still had some students who did not want to behave and every once in a while had to assign lunch detention or call parents.

I also had a few extreme cases of misbehavior that I tried to handle by using a behavior contract that I called the Behavior Support Plan. I found a time to talk to the student privately, usually during my planning period or lunch, and we identified his or her misbehaviors and came up with strategies to improve his or her behavior. For example, I had one student with extreme anger-management issues such that, when he became angry, it was like a volcanic eruption. He needed some serious counseling. When I pulled him aside during lunch, he filled out his behavior plan and admitted that he needed to work on his anger. He wrote in his plan that he would work on his behavior by writing a note to me if he got mad or by asking to meet with me in the hallway. He also wrote that he would try to ignore the students who were bothering him. We agreed that his rewards could be a homework pass, candy, or something to do with football. He mentioned that he liked the Indianapolis Colts. The last two parts of the contract were preventive measures and consequences. As a preventive measure, he agreed to take a time-out if he felt that he was getting upset, and we designated a place in the classroom for that. The consequences were the same as they were for everyone else—lunch detention, parent conference, and referral. Sometimes he received a reward, but other times he received a consequence. The behavior contract idea was not perfect; sometimes it worked, and sometimes he didn't care.

I continued to struggle with the lack of follow-through from the administration, the same two administrators from the previous year. In addition to the intervention logs, I used my own time to initiate a behavior contract and go through the process with a student, and when a student still decided to misbehave, I wrote a referral, as I stated in the contract. I expected the administration to take action, but nothing ever happened, and my efforts in developing a behavior contract were not even acknowledged. The administrators had the same discipline approach that they had had the year before: do nothing. I was just grateful that I did not have any classes like that infamous fourth-period class.

The teachers from India had a rough time teaching at Mayewood. The students shouted and sang while Mr. Mekela was trying to teach, carried on conversations, and ignored him. The principal and the assistant principal would go into the classroom, not to help, but to document all the things he was doing wrong. The problem was that the administration could not control the classes either because they had allowed the students to misbehave and had ignored Mr. Mekala's pleads for help. I felt sorry for him as his face went from cheerful and happy at the beginning of the year to depressed, sad, and disillusioned.

He talked about the respect of the students and the appreciation for education in India, and then one day Mr. Brown was in Mr. Mekala's room, and he was gone. He had been fired before the Thanksgiving break. I was sad that I did not get to say goodbye to him, but later on in the school year Mrs. Dasyum told Mr. Mekela where all the teachers were planning to go to dinner, and he made a surprise appearance. He told us that he was working in a different school district and that the kids were much better.

I wondered who would be brave enough to fill Mr. Mekela's position after the kids had been out of control for so long. Substitute after substitute came to the school, the students treated the subs the same way they had treated Mr. Mekala, and the administration could do nothing because they did not have control of the situation. The subs came and went, never to return. One substitute, who was a retired teacher, commented that she wasn't paid enough to put up with the disrespect and asked to be taken off the sub list at Mayewood.

Until they found a long-term sub able to withstand the challenge, Mr. Brown filled the position. Mr. Brown was a Jack-of-all-trades. If he was needed in the lunchroom, he was there. If he was needed in the computer lab, he was there. If a teacher needed someone to escort a student out of class or the teacher needed a bathroom break, he was there. In addition to driving one of the school buses, he was the football and basketball coach. He knew where most of the kids lived because of his bus route. He knew most of the students' parents or guardians and was respected in the community, so most students would not disrespect him or misbehave the way they did with the subs and Mr. Mekela. On a few occasions, a student tried to test him by misbehaving while he was teaching, but Mr. Brown had a way of turning the situation around so the class was laughing at the misbehaving student. This made the student think twice before he tried anything again. Some of the students acted up around Mr. Brown, and he didn't come down on them for everything, but there was a line that they did not cross with him. I asked Mr. Brown why he did not become a teacher, and he said, "They couldn't pay me enough money Mrs. Wright." After Christmas break, they found a long-term sub willing to accept the challenge.

Mrs. Akers-Epps was a long-term substitute from Brewington Academy. Brewington was the alternative school for Sumter School District 2, so she knew what she was about to get herself into at Mayewood. In many ways, Mayewood felt like an alternative school.

The sixth-graders were bragging that they had been the reason for Mr. Mekela's departure, so the seventh- and eighth-graders tried to get their Indian teachers fired as well. The eighth-grade students terrorized Mrs. Shaik. They threw things at her. They ripped and vandalized her posters and other things she had on the wall and on her desk. They stole things out of her room. They talked and ignored her while she taught. Like Mr. Mekela, she received no support from the administration, but unlike Mr. Mekela, she was not sad; she was angry, and she took a stand for her own self-respect and quit. I was not surprised that she quit, just surprised that it happened so suddenly. I did not get a chance to say goodbye to her and never saw or heard from her again. I guess Mrs. Shaik was not about to go twelve rounds and then suffer a TKO from the administration like Mr. Mekela had. She knew how it would end, so she quit before they could fire her.

The eighth graders felt that they had won some sort of victory, so they bragged like the sixth-graders had until Ms. V. Prince, a retired teacher, replaced Mrs. Shaik. She had an anecdote for everything, and the students thought she was crazy so no one dared to mess with her.

Now the only Indian teacher left was Mrs. Dasyum, the seventh-grade teacher. Mrs. Dasyum knew the fate of the other two teachers and was determined to go the distance. She worked with Mrs. Moses-Polk, the math coach, to develop engaging lesson plans. She watched Mrs. Moses-Polk and Kelly teach lessons and tried to model their techniques. She worked late and came in early to plan lessons and activities that would engage the students. I think the administration must have been taking heat for the loss of two teachers in one school year because they actually started trying to help Mrs. Dasyum and sometimes even removed disruptive students from her class and sent them to ISS. Mrs. Moses-Polk and the administrators often sat in during the worst class periods, not to compile evidence her, but to determine the root of the problem and help her get through the school year. The administration decided that if she had better lesson plans, the students would behave differently, but that wasn't the case; the mission of most of the students was not to learn but to get Mrs. Dasyum fired or make her quit.

The administrators then blamed Mrs. Dasyum for her lack of classroom management skills and refused to admit that they could have done a better job supporting her and the other two teachers from the beginning. How is someone from another country, where classroom discipline is not an issue, supposed to know how to manage unruly and disrespectful students? They went through the new teacher induction classes, but talking about classroom management and experiencing it are two different things, especially when you don't have administrative support.

Mrs. Dasyum's initial reaction to her mistreatment was different from that of Mr. Mekela and Mrs. Shaik. She was not sad or angry; she was frustrated, she wanted to know what she had to do to get the students to learn, and she wanted to be a successful teacher in the United States. She knew that the students were trying to get rid of her as they had done to her colleagues, but she refused to allow them their victory. She was a strong-willed, determined, and persistent fighter, and I admired her. Eventually, the students realized that if they were disruptive, they risked the chance of being sent to ISS and isolated from their friends for the rest of the day. They were also intimidated by the increased presence of the administrators, who were clearly observing them, not the teacher. Mrs. Dasyum's perseverance paid off because the students eventually lost interest in chasing her off. There were still some bad apples, but the majority of her classes settled down. She made it through the entire school year, but she did not return the next year. She transferred to a high school in the district, which she said she loved, and the kids behaved better. Mrs. Shaik moved to a different state. I heard that she and Mr. Mekela enjoyed their new schools and that their students and administrations treated them better.

One day we were told that the state Department of Education's External Review Team would be visiting Mayewood because we had received an "unsatisfactory" rating in academic performance. Their job was to evaluate what was going on at the school and determine which strategies and professional development courses should be implemented to improve student progress.

They visited in December. I made sure my standards and agenda were written clearly on the board. I had my lesson plan book opened and on my desk, ready for their visit to my class.

The External Review Team consisted of three people, Mr. M, Ms. W, and Ms. O. They set up shop in a small conference room in the media center, and for four days they walked around the school with their clipboards and checklists. They visited different classrooms each day, stopped teachers and students in the hallway to ask questions, and met with parents and students to ask questions.

My first classroom visit came from Mr. M, who had his clipboard and checklist. He started looking around my classroom, but he stopped when he reached the back of the room and started observing my class. I was nervous, but I was happy because he had walked in on a PowerPoint presentation. He stayed in my class for a few minutes and watched me teach the lesson. I was proud of my students, as they raised their hands, and they were very active and focused on the lesson. (You would have thought that I bribed them, but like me, they were just trying to impress him.) Before he left, he told me I had done a nice job with my PowerPoint presentation and asked me if I did them often. Those were the first encouraging words I had heard from someone other than a colleague. The administration never said anything encouraging to me; I always felt unappreciated by the administration and beat up emotionally by the students, so Mr. M's positive comments made me feel good.

At the end of the four days, Ms. B came to my classroom. I wasn't nervous anymore, but she came during a boring lesson, as we were reviewing for a test. She stayed for a few minutes and left. I saw her later on that day, and she complimented me on my classroom management. I don't need to be complimented all the time, but when you are used to hearing only negative comments and you finally hear something positive, it's encouraging and motivating. Ms. O never came to my room.

What I will never forget about their visit was the interview with our sixth-grade team. Each grade-level team had to meet with the group from the ERT in the small conference room in the media center. The eighth-grade team went the day prior to our meeting, so I asked Kelly what it was like, and she told me that they just asked questions about the school.

On the sixth-grade team's day to meet with the group, we walked into the small room and sat in the chairs at the other end of the conference table from where the ERT members were seated. They had their clipboards and checklists, and we all introduced ourselves. They already knew everything they wanted to know about us because they had access to everything—teacher files, student files, whatever they wanted. Then they each took turns asking questions of the group, and whoever wanted to answer had their chance to speak. Believe me, we spoke our minds.

"What is it like teaching here at Mayewood?" asked Mr. M.

"Do you feel safe here?" asked Ms. B.

"Describe student behavior in the classroom," requested Ms. O.

"Tell me about your school improvement plan," said Mr. M.

We looked at them, then at each other, and replied, "What improvement plan?"

"How are you treated by the administration?" asked Ms. O. This question opened the ultimate therapy session, and everyone spoke their minds because, like the year before, the administration did not support us the way we needed them to support us. I remember thinking how Mr. Mekala, the now former sixth-grade math teacher, was one of their casualties. Later on, the ERT members met with the principal and assistant principal. When the four days were over, the trio from the state's Department of Education packed up and went back to present their findings about Mayewood Middle School.

The next day we found a packet in our mailboxes entitled "School Improvement Plan." I thought, "Oh, this is what the trio was talking about." It was funny that we should have already had this document but the administrators had kept it to themselves. Another surprise was how the principal and assistant principal suddenly became more involved with student discipline, cracking down on student behavior. I guess the trio mentioned to the superintendent or the administrators how the teachers at Mayewood, not just the sixth-grade team, felt they did not get administrative support.

However, we had won only a small battle because later the support faded and the war was on.

The first thing was our bulletin boards. During one of our staff meetings, the principal said she had noticed that teachers were not updating their bulletin boards, and she walked around the school doing bulletin board checks. If she had focused on improving student behavior the way she focused on our bulletin boards, we might have had fewer discipline problems in our classrooms.

After the bulletin board issue got old, she found other little things to harass us about. Once she came into my room, unannounced, for at least twenty-five minutes, walking in with the students at the beginning of first period. I handed her my lessons, and she sat down and started her surprise observation. It was great! The students came in, did their warm-up, and then read silently. We went over the warm-up and moved quickly into the lesson I had planned for the day. Halfway into the lesson, she quietly walked out. During my planning period that day, I was sitting at my desk grading papers when the principal walked in. I just knew she was going to say something complimentary because everything had gone perfectly during her surprise visit: my students were active and participating, I had no behavior issues, I was teaching a good lesson, and I had even shown her my lesson plan book. I just knew that she was about to say something encouraging.

Wrong.

She said, "Mrs. Wright, did you know the analogy that you had for number two was wrong?"

I said, "Yes, Mrs. X, I realized that and changed it before second period."

She replied, "Okay," and left.

I could not believe it! The only thing she could say to me was something negative. I was so disillusioned that I couldn't even grade papers anymore. I went to Kelly's classroom and told her what had happened, and she couldn't believe it either. I officially hated being at Mayewood.

The drama did not stop there. The principal and the assistant principal decided to mess with my second-year evaluation.

My first year evaluations had been okay. I wasn't cited for any major problems other than classroom management, but I knew I had tried my best in that area; I just hadn't had the administrative support I needed. However, the second-year evaluation was a nightmare.

The principal and the assistant principal had come to my room twice during the year and collected data, and then we had a meeting in which they shared their findings with me. I was a little nervous, but I knew that the evaluation was going to be good because I had improved significantly compared to the year before. The briefing took place in the principal's office. The assistant principal sat in the principal's chair, and the principal stood beside her while I sat in a chair by the door that faced her desk. This was obviously the assistant principal's show, and she started off by saying some good things—how I used a timer and moved around the classroom—but the way she spoke let me know that this was a set-up and, boy, was I right. She quickly moved into the realm of the not-so-positive:

1. Lesson plans need to be complete. (It was true that I had stopped writing out every little detail on my lesson plans since the curriculum was the same as it had been the year before, and I knew the concepts I wanted to teach and how I was going to teach them. I wrote down only the standards, agenda, and a brief outline.)

2. Information presented orally. Use overhead to provide content and directions visually.

3. More student work needs to be displayed.

4. Teacher yells at students when they don't comply with her instructions.

If I had been a cartoon, steam would have been coming from my ears. I was so upset that I began to cry. I could not believe what I was hearing. I can take constructive criticism, but when someone writes lies and falsehoods about me that go on my professional record, as points 2 and 4 were, it's infuriating.

I went straight to the district office and told Mr. Wilson how flabbergasted I was about their comments. I also wrote a rebuttal to refute points 2 and 4. I had worked hard that year, and this evaluation was upsetting. Number 2 showed that they were out of touch because I frequently used PowerPoint presentations to accompany my lessons, and there was no mention of these presentations. This was the most disheartening comment because the teaching strategies I implemented and how I incorporated technology into my lesson plans were completely unnoticed by the administration. Number 4 angered me the most because she made me sound like I was some psychopath drill sergeant. I had learned from my first year that I could not have a friendly tone; I was a nice teacher, but I gave commands instead of requests, saying, for example, "Put your pencils away and clear your desk" instead of "would you please put your pencils away and clear your desk?" My principal wanted me to have a more friendly tone, but my students responded to commands, not requests, and if I had been too friendly, they would have run all over me. She did not understand that because she was not in the classroom with them all day.

Mr. Wilson, the principal, the assistant principal, and I met to discuss my evaluation. I gave them each a copy of my rebuttal and told them that the evaluation did not fairly represent me as a teacher. Of course, the principal and assistant principal acted like they were shocked that their comments had offended me, but they pretended to care only because Mr. Wilson was in the room. The assistant principal told me that her comment about my interactions with students was not based on her observations but on a student's statement. I expressed my concern about her decision to put this on my permanent teaching record based on what one student said instead of talking to me about the situation, as this student had been angry with me because I would not let him extend his lunch into the second lunch period.

Here's what had happened: The student reported to lunch about fifteen minutes late because he was waiting for someone to drop off clothes he needed for an after-school activity. He came into the lunchroom, ate his lunch, and talked with his friends, but when the lunch period was over, he demanded that he be allowed to stay for second lunch because he was at lunch for only fifteen minutes. When I declined his request because he had already finished eating and he just wanted to play around with his friends, he became angry and ranted that students were supposed to have thirty minutes for lunch and he had had only fifteen minutes. I told him that it had been his decision to wait in the office for his clothes and reminded him that he had already finished eating his lunch, but he said he wanted to order another lunch because he was still hungry. As we were lining the students up to go back to class, he saw the assistant principal and pleaded his case. Although I informed her that he had already eaten lunch and that he only wanted to be with his friends in seventh grade, she overruled my decision. I couldn't believe it. After that, every time this student disagreed with me, he said he was going to talk to the assistant principal. She took some of my power away that day. This is the student she said made the comment about my yelling at students. We ended the meeting with an agreement to have a better line of communication between the administration and myself.

To this day, I feel that this was a vindictive evaluation, but I never knew why. What I did know was that I could no longer handle being at Mayewood. If I stayed, I probably wouldn't be a teacher much longer.

After my evaluation nightmare, I was on a mission to find another place to work. I sent out my resume and went through the application process with Clarendon School District 2 and Richland School Districts 1 and 2. Then good news came: I was moving.

My husband decided that he wanted to join the United States Air Force Honor Guard, an elite unit that performed high-profile jobs in and around the nation's capital. He filled out an application, which should have been called a binder portfolio because it had twelve tabs full of information about him, and mailed it to the USAF Honor Guard Headquarters. Then in February 2005, he received an e-mail telling him that he was a new member of the USAF Honor Guard, so we would be moving to Bolling AFB in Washington, DC, in the summer. I was happy for him but just as happy for myself because this meant that I did not have to return to Mayewood. I was going to be free from that place!

After I found out we were moving, the school year flew by. Things that used to bother me didn't bother me anymore. Rhonda was just as happy as I was, if not more, because she had a new social studies teacher position lined up in another school district and would not be returning to Mayewood either. It was like we were prisoners about to be paroled. She cleaned out her classroom closet and filing cabinets and gave me all of her literature and grammar posters since she had decided to teach only social studies. I gladly accepted them and increased my classroom collection.

After I found out we would be moving, I began printing off recommendation forms and teacher applications to work in Maryland. I applied to the Howard County, Montgomery County, and Prince George's County school districts and applied for a Maryland teaching certificate. I was excited. Where would I start my new teaching adventure?

Then the call came. With only a few days left before Spring Break, we had extended our lunchtime and taken the students outside for some free time. I was sitting on the bleachers with the other sixth-grade teachers when I received a call from Montgomery County Public School District's Human Resources Department asking me to come in for an interview.

In April, we visited Maryland and Washington, DC for a few days, during which I went to the district office and met with Rochelle Kraus, the staffing coordinator. She began with the quintessential question, "Why do you want to be a teacher?" and asked me to talk about my past teaching experiences.

I told her about my experiences at the Academic Learning Center and how I had grown as a teacher at Mayewood. Before I handed her my evaluation forms from Mayewood, I explained that I did not have a very good relationship with my principal and that I was not very satisfied at my present job, but I never let that stop me from being the best teacher possible. I was completely honest with her, and when the interview was over, she all but told me "welcome aboard" and that representatives from different schools would be contacting me to set up interviews.

I couldn't believe how much easier the process was compared to my previous hiring experiences. I went through so much drama when I moved to South Carolina, and now I didn't even have to worry about acquiring a Maryland teaching certificate. (I guess it showed up in the system that I had already applied for my Maryland certificate because I was told that I did not have to worry about anymore paperwork or fees associated with it because they had a department that handled that information.) It was a completely different hiring experience. I didn't know if having two teaching certificates and two years of teaching experience made a difference, but it didn't matter because I was just glad that things were going smoothly. Now all I had to do was wait for the principals to start calling.

However, after a few weeks had gone by, I still had not heard from any principals. I was becoming doubtful and wondered whether anyone was going to call me. Then I finally received a call from the principal of North Bethesda Middle School, and the next day I received calls from Mark Twain Middle School and Francis Scott Key Middle School. There I had been, questioning whether anyone was going to call, and then the calls wouldn't stop. Instead of having faith, I was full of doubt. (I later discovered that the principals could not start calling teacher candidates until after a certain date.)

One of the last people to call was Jean Tufano, who was in charge of the English Department at Tilden Middle School. She was different from the other callers because she wanted to do a telephone interview before deciding to have a face-to-face meeting. She asked me a few questions, and I asked her some questions. By the end of our conversation, I was sold, and she told me that she would love for me to be a part of the staff at Tilden. I did not want to waste anyone's time, so I called the other schools and cancelled the scheduled interviews. I couldn't wait to see what was in store for me at my new school, but I had to finish the current school year at Mayewood.

One of the last units in the curriculum guide was about drama, and I wanted the students to perform a play in class. The on-level and TAG (talented and gifted) curricula were different, as time was allotted for a reading and performing the play *Charlie and the Chocolate Factory* in TAG but not in the on-level classes. I wanted to rectify this inequity by developing a script for the on-level students or by having the students write their own script, but I did not have the time because I had to stay with the pace of the curriculum. Then one night, as I read *Jack and the Beanstalk* with my kids, I decided to put on a school-wide production of *Jack and the Beanstalk*. I typed up a script and added my own twist to the story; Jack would take his homeboy Kenny with him when he climbed the beanstalk, and the giants would be Jamaicans.

I presented the idea to the principal, and I was surprised when she loved the idea. For the first time in almost two years, she gave me a compliment. The students were also open to the idea, and a few days after getting the principal's approval, I held auditions. I asked Rhonda to help me choose the students who would perfectly portray each character and told the students about the cast of characters needed for the play. Then the students told me which character they wanted to portray, and I gave them each a copy of a scene from the play. All of the students who auditioned were great, and the cast was complete. We had four weeks to practice, which we did on the stage in the gym where we would perform the play. There was no budget, so we didn't have the best props in the world, but we included enough clues for the audience to understand the setting of each scene.

When the night of the performance arrived, only one month of school remained, so the principal invited the upcoming sixth graders and their parents, which packed the gym. I had never seen so many parents attend any event at Mayewood as attended that night, and I overheard someone who had worked at Mayewood for years comment that she had never seen so many parents and students turn out for any event. The cast members were nervous, as was I.

The cords that were supposed to open and close the curtains did not function properly, so students who wanted to help became the stage crew, running back and forth to open and close the curtains. The play opened with Kenny and Jack talking trash to each other while they played basketball, Jack's mom calling him to come home, and Jack selling his cow. The girl who played the cow was hilarious because of her sassy attitude, and when Jack sold her to the Magic Man, she made a sassy "moo" sound. Next, Jack and Kenny pretended to climb the beanstalk while the stage crew closed the curtains.

We then changed the scene to look like someone's kitchen by putting a dining room table in the center of the stage. The stage crew opened the curtains to reveal Jack and Kenny tiptoeing around the giant's kitchen. They spotted the goose that laid golden eggs, but as they were about to grab it, a female giant walked into the kitchen and they ran for cover. As the giantess prepared lunch, a Reggae song by Bob Marley began to play, and the male giant Reggae-danced his way into the kitchen. While the giants ate lunch, Jack and Kenny stole the goose, but the giant spotted them as they were leaving.

Kenny told Jack to climb down the beanstalk while he distracted the giant, and Kenny sang "Can't Touch This" by M.C. Hammer as he did the hammer dance while Jack escaped down the beanstalk. The irritated giant chased Kenny around the stage until Kenny ran back to the beanstalk. Kenny climbed down the beanstalk to where Jack was waiting at the bottom with his ax. After Jack chopped the beanstalk down and the giant fell, Jack showed his mom what he and Kenny had retrieved from the clouds, and they began to dance and sing, "We're Rich, We're Rich."

The audience reacted most to the dancing Jamaican giant and Kenny's hammer dance, and they commented that seeing the little feet run back and forth to open and close the curtains was cute. The play was a success! Even though I didn't have time for my on-level students to perform a play in class, at least they were able to see a play, and some of them were in the cast.

What I was going to miss the most about Mayewood was the bond that I had formed with the teachers and staff members. We might not always have agreed with each other or even liked each other, but we always worked together and supported each other.

Toward the end of the school year, I was packing up my classroom and thinking about how much I had grown as a teacher. I had stepped straight into the fire, and now I was prepared for anything. I had learned classroom management techniques and the importance of establishing routines, rules, and consequences. I had learned that if you don't have the support of your administrators, your job is ten times harder than it should be. However, the most beneficial thing I learned was that, when teachers work together and form bonds, it makes things a little easier. The glue that held us together was that we were all dealing with some type of student or administrator issue, so we felt each other's pain. I might have hated working at Mayewood, but I have never regretted the teaching experience or the friendships that were established.

At the end of the year, I received my final overall evaluation, which was marked "professional."

Chapter Four

My New School

We finally moved to Washington, DC, in July 2005. The first thing that went wrong was getting lost in rush hour traffic, stuck on I-495 while towing our second car. We were looking for the exit to the hotel that would be our home until we received base housing, but we could not find the right exit, so we went up I-495 and down I-495. Thank goodness for the DVD feature in our Expedition because we did not hear a peep from the kids!

We had never seen so many cars. It was like a massive parking lot, and we moved inches at a time. When we finally found the right exit, went to the hotel to prepare for the next day; I was going to visit my new school.

The next morning we got up early to go to Tilden Middle School. Our first encounter with this interstate was not very positive, so I dreaded getting back on it. We left around 9:30, and traffic was not as bad as the previous day. When we finally made it to Tilden, my family and I met Jean in the front office. We shook hands, and she showed me around the school. She introduced me to the office staff and the principal and then she told me my room would be D113 in the D wing, and we headed there. She showed me her room and the storage closet where all the literature books and novels were located and then the English office, where all the materials I needed were located.

I looked around me in shock. I did not have to buy my own pencils, pens, and other school materials. They even had the good pens and not the cheap ones.

After touring the school, we shook hands again and my family and I headed back to the hotel. After seeing the school and meeting the people, I was happy with my decision.

When August 14, 2006, rolled around, I went to Montgomery County's New Educator's Orientation to become familiar with the ways of Montgomery County School District. It was a three-day seminar that all teachers new to the county had to attend, whether you were a new teacher or had twenty years of experience. I learned about the curriculum and some of the strategies I was expected to use in my classroom, such as a plus/delta chart and a comment section. The plus/delta chart was used to get feedback on what worked and what needed improvement, and the comment section was a designated location in the classroom where students could leave feedback or questions about a lesson if they were afraid to ask a question or make a comment in front of the class.

The next week I had to report to Tilden. Of course, I got there early and set up my classroom, as I knew from experience that teachers were not given enough time in their classrooms during in-service days to set up and plan lessons. There was a perfect spot in my classroom for my reading area. During the meetings, I felt overwhelmed because I received so many handouts, along with several binders that contained the curriculum for my English and reading classes. I was assigned two sixth-grade English classes, two sixth-grade reading classes, and one seventh-grade intervention reading class. Jean apologized because my schedule had three preps and no GT (Gifted and Talented) classes, and she explained that the teacher before me had requested that schedule, but he had not returned to Tilden because he had taken another job. I told her that I didn't mind having that schedule; I survived Mayewood so I could survive anything.

During the training sessions, I met Kim, an eighth-grade English teacher in the special education department. We connected right away. If I did not understand something about the curriculum or if I had questions about Tilden or Montgomery County Public Schools, I went to her because she had been teaching in the county for six years which included being at Tilden for two years. She was my "go to" person. I also met my sixth-grade team members: Len and Laila taught social studies; Susie and Dawn taught English and reading; Penny and Leslie taught math; and Kelly and Mary Ellen taught science. Laila and Mary Ellen were the sixth-grade team leaders. This was a much larger team than the Mayewood sixth-grade team so I would have to learn many more personalities. One day during the pre-service week, we had a team lunch for which I had received a nice, handcrafted invitation in my mailbox that instructed me to bring my own drink. My new team was very organized: We met in the team room, where there were two pie pans of quiche, salad, and rolls. I had never heard of quiche before that day, but I was willing to try anything.

Not only did I have to adjust to a new school, I also had to adjust to dealing with traffic. I was used to hopping in my car and driving to work, not moving a few inches forward every five minutes. I told Laurie, the English para-educator, how I was frustrated about the time I was wasting in traffic (my commute was a minimum forty five minutes one way), and she suggested I get a few of my favorite CDs and sing along with them. Her advice worked. I would listen to Smooth Jazz 105.9, which was calming. Laurie worked with me during first period, which was great because if I were delayed by accidents or other delays in traffic, she would be there to carry out the morning routine for me. She was also great at helping me to stay organized.

When the first day of school arrived, I immediately noticed a difference in student behavior from what I had experienced at Mayewood. They were quiet and polite, looking up at me like baby birds waiting for their mother to feed them. They were ready to learn and I was ready to teach them. After we established the routines, the students would walk in quietly and begin working on their journals. My first-period and last-period classes were heavenly, the perfect way to begin and end the day.

My seventh-grade intervention reading class was different from my sixth-grade reading class in that it was a small class of ten students. They were good students, but some of them resented being in the intervention class because it required them to use one of their elective choices. Since this was not a class that they would have voluntarily selected, there were times when they were not motivated to do their work. In addition, I was not able to use my classroom because the reading intervention class required a specific arrangement that meant I had to go upstairs to Claudia's classroom. I did not like having to carry my stuff upstairs or being in another teacher's space. Claudia insisted that I make myself at home in her classroom, but I was still reluctant to change anything to suit my needs.

Claudia was very knowledgeable about this program because she had been a coordinator for three years, and she was an asset to me both inside and outside the classroom. She showed me how to manage the reading intervention program and work in small groups with the students, and she made me feel welcome in her classroom. (Some teachers don't like to share their space, but she was the opposite.) Even though I felt welcome, I still did not want to rearrange things in her room, but she told me to take whatever materials I needed out of her closet. She was one of those seasoned teachers who made a noticeable difference in student achievement. By the time a student had finished her class, he or she was reading two or three grade levels above where he or she started.

Claudia was also a very thoughtful person who knew that three preps was tough, and she saw that I was becoming frustrated. One day she inquired about my favorite type of candy, and I told her that I loved Twix bars, of which I had sold out the snack machine on a few occasions. A few days later, I found a bag of Twix bars with an encouraging note in my mailbox. She often said things to encourage me, and every once in a while surprised me with thoughtful gifts and words to remind me to hang in there. I love and respect Claudia, and I am forever grateful for her kindness.

In November, I received a pre-observation sheet in my mailbox. It was time for midyear evaluations, so Jean and I examined our schedules and determined the best time for her to observe one of my classes. I was nervous when she arrived in my third-period class because she had hired me and I did not want her to regret her decision. My lesson pertained to Greek mythology, which was the focus of the curriculum at that time. My evaluation went smoothly; Jean commented about my incorrect pronunciation of "Hephaestus," but my evaluation was successful overall.

December rolled around, and I updated my bulletin board to fit the season, as I had for October and November. I purchased baby blue fabric with tiny Christmas trees, but I soon realized that I had underestimated the length of the board. I would have to wait until the weekend to go back to Walmart. (That's one thing I missed about being in South Carolina; Walmart was in convenient locations.)

On Wednesday of that week, I found Mr. Easton, the assistant principal, standing outside of my classroom. He rarely came to my end of the hallway, and I was thinking about anything I could have done wrong that would warrant a visit from him. When I walked up to him, he told me that I could not use the fabric that was on my bulletin board because Christmas trees were Christian symbols that were not inclusive of Jewish students and teachers. I was fine with that decision until I learned that a teacher in my hallway had complained to him about the fabric. I was upset because I am a very approachable person, and that teacher could have easily explained how Tilden had a large Jewish population and that my fabric might offend or exclude someone. As I was taking down the fabric, I asked myself how I was supposed to bond with these teachers if they felt that they could not approach me about a bulletin board. Susie, the other sixth-grade English and reading teacher and my mentor, made me feel better about this situation one morning when she gave me a green gift bag containing three Christmas-tree-shaped ornaments. I still have them, and I think about her when I put them on my tree every Christmas.

Christmas vacation finally arrived. The first half of the year had been great, but things were about to change. During the break, I received a call from Jean, who told me that Dawn would not be returning because she had decided to stay home with her baby; she had had the baby in November, and her "gifted and talented" (GT) students had had various substitutes since then. The GT parents complained about the subs and demanded that their kids have a certified teacher. That lucky teacher was me, and that meant I would be teaching two GT classes.

After we returned from the break, I had new third-period and fourth-period classes. It was a little heartbreaking since I had just started forming relationships with my students, and now they had another teacher. I had to go through my rules and procedures again, which I had already established with my previous students, and I had to revamp my lesson plans to accommodate the GT students. My new fourth period did not like the change either, as they had already adjusted to their previous teacher's rules and procedures, and now they had to adjust to me. These students were resistant and did not like having a new teacher, so some of them were rude to me. One student, who had decided he was the class spokesperson, started a petition against me, but he didn't know that I didn't want his class either! After a class conference with the principal and several parent phone calls, the behaviors calmed down, but they never went away.

My new third-period class was another monster. These students had had various subs for at least a month, and they were accustomed to doing very little work. The parents had complained about their children not having a certified teacher, but with a certified teacher come real grades, and the parents did not like those real grades. After third-quarter interims, I started receiving e-mails from parents demanding to know why their children had been given a certain grade, and these were not nice e-mails. I began to dread opening my e-mail, and each time I logged in, I asked myself how much hate mail would I receive that day. Most of these e-mails were from parents who knew their children should not be in a GT class, even though they had. This bothered me because these parents demanded that their children be placed in GT against their previous teacher's recommendation.

Most of the parents were simply looking for a way to blame me instead of working together to find ways to help their children be successful in my class. One parent, whose daughter fell into this category, requested a parent conference because her daughter had a low C average in my class. We met during my planning period, and I showed her the work that her daughter produced and the work that was expected of a GT student. We talked about extra work she could do to improve her skills, and I told her that I was available during lunch and morning academic period (MAP) to meet with her daughter. I thought the conference went well, but the mom contacted the principal and Jean to demand another conference that included them. She wrote a rude and hostile e-mail stating that her daughter did not deserve a C in my class, and she didn't understand how she had had a B for the first two quarters and now a low C in my class.

I was ready for this conference. I had student work samples to compare her daughter's work with a GT student's work. I printed out the e-mails that we exchanged before this conference to show my principal that I had contacted the parent and tried to work with her. At the beginning of the conference, the parent was aggressive and angry. Again, I compared an assignment her daughter had produced with a GT student's assignment. Like Rhonda from Mayewood would say, "You can't fit a square peg in a round hole." The conference went great for me because I had all my ducks in a row. My principal supported me when the parent tried to say that I was the reason her daughter had a C average, and the parent's attitude had changed by the end of the conference. From that day on, I vowed never again to teach GT classes at Tilden. Jean told me not to judge all GT classes by these two, but I did.

Toward the end of the school year, teachers were allowed to request the classes they preferred to teach during the next school year. I requested sixth-grade on-level English and reading classes, omitting the seventh-grade class because I did not want three preps. Jean insisted that I give GT another try, but I told her that I really preferred on-level classes.

Overall, this was a good year. It was my first time teaching with novels, which was challenging and fun, and I enjoyed having a mixed population of students. I received my first-year evaluation, and it was checked "professional."

Since the school year was coming to a close, my students helped me put textbooks and the books in the reading area in my classroom closet. Susie suggested that I write my name and room number on all of the desks, tables, and chairs in my classroom so they would make it back into my classroom after my room was cleaned in the summer, and the students helped me tape and label all the furniture. Susie also told me that it was tradition for all the teachers to walk out to the buses with the students on the last day of school and wave goodbye. On the last day of school, I walked out with the other teachers and happily waved goodbye to the students and to another school year.

Chapter Five

Do I Really Want This?

My second year at Tilden started, as usual, with a pre-service week. Since I did not have to pack everything up at the end of the prior year, setting up my room was very easy. This year was also my last evaluation year for the next five years.

Jean moved up to the high-school level to teach English, so Regina, an English teacher from another middle school, was the new leader of the English department. Leslie moved to another school to become a math specialist so Emily became the new math teacher. There was also a new principal at Tilden, whose name was Jennifer. She was very supportive and willing to listen to ideas, and she was also visible. I never saw the previous principal unless I went to the front office, but Jennifer could be seen all over the school; you never knew when she was going to pop up. She was a welcome change to my experience with principals.

My friendship with Kim had grown stronger. Sometimes I dreaded going to Kim for advice because she always told me what I needed to hear, not what I wanted to hear. She was always a by-the-book person; and while I'm not a rebel, sometimes I'm willing to take a risk. For example, I once received a long, nasty e-mail from a parent who was angry because his daughter turned a homework assignment in late and I gave her half credit, which was county policy. I wanted to reply to him the way he addressed me—rude and nasty—but I typed my response in as calm and respectful a tone as possible. I sent it to Kim for her opinion, and she told me not to send it. I guess my feelings were too obvious. Before she helped me with revisions, I told her that I was tired of being disrespected and talked to like I was nothing, and I was ready to fight back. With her heavy Trinidadian accent she said, "I know, I know, Sylvia. But you can't send this." I did not want to listen, but I did. She convinced me it wasn't worth the risk, and she told me that the parent was probably just taking out his frustrations on me. I revised the e-mail and sent it. Kim was always my voice of reason. This year, Armecia, a seventh-grade English teacher, joined our little circle.

Overall, the students this year were nice and respectful. My fourth-period class was my largest—and liveliest—class. This was the first class after lunch, so they always had a tough time settling down, and there was always some type of drama happening between two or more of them. Two students in the class in particular, who had a love-hate relationship, always found something to argue about. I separated them to the far ends of the class, but every once in a while they still managed to get into some type of loud altercation. This was annoying because most of the students from fourth period were also in my fifth-period class, so I had to tolerate this lively and dramatic class for ninety minutes straight. Fortunately, my sixth period was planning and my seventh period was heavenly.

The year started out fine, but the more it progressed, the more depressed I became. It started during the second quarter. Regina, the English leader, came to evaluate me before my final evaluation, and I was anxious. She observed one of my reading classes in which I introduced Greek mythology. I thought the lesson had gone well, but I completely misjudged myself. Based on Regina's evaluation comments, I was a below-standard teacher. I spoke with another teacher about the comments on my evaluation form, and she showed me the book that is used for evaluations, and most of the comments Regina had listed on my evaluation were copied straight from the "below standard" column of the *Teacher Evaluation Handbook*. I was distraught.

I am sometimes a perfectionist, so this hit me in the gut. As usual, Kim was my therapist, and she told me to ask Regina what I could do to improve, but I did not want to speak to Regina. Instead, I acted like one of my sixth-graders. If I saw her walking down the hall, I changed directions so I wouldn't encounter her directly. I eventually grew up and asked Regina what I could do to improve, but she did not give me a clear answer. (I have always believed that if you tell someone she did something incorrectly, then you should be able to tell her how to make the corrections.) Regina eventually asked me for the questions I had used during the lesson, and she showed me how to make the questions more rigorous.

I began to put the pieces of the puzzle together: Regina was evaluating me based on the level of rigor in my classes because "rigor" was the key word in the new Middle School Reform Initiative that was taking place that year throughout MCPS. Since there were no specific evaluation guidelines for an evaluation of "rigor," she had used the regular evaluation guidelines to judge how rigorous I was as a teacher.

Rigor refers to how you challenge your students' minds, but I usually created questions that required students to use the lower levels of Bloom's Taxonomy—knowledge, comprehension, and application—and rarely required students to use the higher-order thinking skills of analysis, synthesis, and evaluation. I began to create questions that made students evaluate what they had read, formulate an opinion, and use evidence from the story or passage to support their answers. For example, in the novel, *Where the Red Fern Grows*, a non-rigorous question about the section in which Billy walked to Tahlequah to retrieve his pups would ask how far Billy had to walk to get to Tahlequah, while a more rigorous question would ask what character trait would you give Billy and why? A good answer might say that Billy was determined because he walked twenty miles to get his pups. I recreated questions that required students to evaluate Billy's actions, form an opinion, and support their opinions using proof from the story. Once this light bulb went off in my head, I changed the way I questioned my students. I still used the lower levels of Bloom's Taxonomy to create questions, but I more frequently used higher-level questions than lower-level questions.

Before I began working with Regina to incorporate higher-order thinking questions into my lessons, she told me that she had received several e-mails from parents, some complaining that my class was too easy, and some complaining that my class was too hard. Then she said I did not give enough A grades. Some teachers give students grades, but if a student wants a good grade in my class, he or she has to meet the necessary requirements to earn it. I was taken aback because I had told Regina that students were not turning in homework assignments and not reading their assigned novels—and it was the students who had not done the reading and the homework assignments who scored low. Regina then asked what I was doing to get them to do their work. I told her that I meet with students during MAP, my lunch period, and sometimes after school and that I called and e-mailed parents. Then she told me that my grades were probably not balanced because I taught only on-level classes. (She thought I was crazy for not wanting to teach GT classes.)

After my conference with Regina, I told Wendy, a teacher friend across the hall, what Regina had told me about my performance, and she was as surprised as I had been. I told her that I didn't understand why I was to blame when students refused to do the work I assigned. I had had enough. I wanted out of education.

I never thought I would feel this way. I had tried to motivate my students, but some just didn't want to do their assignments, and I was tired of being the scapegoat for unmotivated students, especially when I revised lessons and made myself available to them if they needed my help. I was so depressed that I forgot why I became a teacher. My life felt mundane and purposeless.

I reformulated my résumé to gear it toward human resources, but when I showed it to Wendy, she laughed—not at me, but at its length. It was really short. I knew how to write a résumé geared toward teaching, but not one for a secretarial position. Wendy gave me some tips, I did some research, and I finally formulated a descent résumé. I did not feel that I had enough tenure in the county school district to get a job outside the classroom, so I applied other places. The first place I applied was the Defense Intelligence Agency because it was near my house on the base. I fantasized about how wonderful it would be to walk to work and not have to commute to Maryland. I also applied for other secretarial jobs that were listed in the *Washington Post*. I was happy. I was escaping the pressure to be a perfect teacher, and I would no longer be blamed for student behavior.

Weeks and then months went by, and I heard nothing. Applying for the government job was a new experience for me because I had to upload my résumé to an employment database that someone had to look through to find my application, and I could not contact a specific person directly. Laila told me that it took years for a friend of hers to be contacted for a government position. I felt trapped again because I could not find an escape.

When fourth quarter was in full swing, there was a happy moment for me when a few students who had not read their novels the past three quarters decided to read their fourth-quarter novel. Their grades improved, and they actively participated in classroom discussions. I was so proud of them. Individually, I asked them why they hadn't performed like this all year, and the general response was "I don't know," although a few students said the other books were boring. I was excited by these improvements, but I had made up my mind that I was getting out of the classroom.

Time was running out, and I had to make a decision to stay in Montgomery County or find another job. Although there was a deadline to inform the county that I planned to leave, I did not want to tell them that I was leaving without having another job lined up. I went back to the *Washington Post* classified ads and found a listing for a school that needed someone to write curriculum. I thought this would be perfect because I could still be in education but would not have to be in a classroom.

When the day of my interview arrived, I was nervous because this was my last chance to get away from the classroom. The assistant principal asked me the usual questions related to what had I experienced throughout my years of teaching. We discussed "what if" scenarios, and then she gave me a tour of the building. After that, she told me I would have to come back and be interviewed by a panel of teachers and the principal and would have to construct a lesson and go into a classroom to model the lesson. I was distraught; I did not have time to go through this process. I remember running to my car because it was raining, and sitting in the driver's seat, crying, both hands over my face. I was so desperate to leave and now I would have to stay in the classroom.

Then I realized that my plan was not God's plan. I was fighting against His will for my life. I was angry about my situation, so I had reacted without thinking; I wanted things my way, but God had other plans for my life.

I told Mary Ellen and Laila that I would be returning, and Mary Ellen smiled, as she had not wanted me to leave.

A few weeks later, the school year was over, and I met with my principal for final checkout. I had agreed to teach two English and two reading classes the next school year and be the coordinator for the Extended Learning Program, which offered after-school classes that reinforced reading and math skills. My job in that role would be to enroll students, hire teachers for the program, and make sure everything ran smoothly.

I was burned out, so I threw everything in my closet and left school for a much-needed summer vacation. As I was leaving, I said to myself that the next year was going to be a better year.

Chapter Six

Will This Be A Better Year?

The 2008-2009 school year rolled around, and I returned with a positive attitude. "This year is going to be a good year!" I repeated to myself and my colleagues, and I believed it. Kim had left to become the head of a special education department at another middle school, and the thought that she would not be at Tilden made me sad, but I knew it was a great career move. She had plans to be an administrator, and this job opportunity moved her one step closer to her goal. Every once in a while, we still got together on the weekend for lunch.

I decided to change my eating habits. I had gained weight during the previous year because I ate fast food whenever I became stressed, and I was stressed a lot. Some days I went to Balducci's and ordered the Sante Fe chicken sandwich, and other days I had two cheeseburgers and large fries or a three piece chicken strip meal with mash potatoes and a biscuit. Whenever I was feeling low, I went out for lunch because I found it soothing. This was becoming a serious problem because I didn't have a serious work-out schedule, and the pounds had begun to accumulate. It wasn't until this year that I began to think seriously about what I ate, and I became more dedicated to working out at the gym.

I decided to try the three-hour diet plan in an effort to eat healthier. Each week I created an eating schedule and ate something every three hours, starting with breakfast at 6:00 a.m. For breakfast, I ate yogurt, a banana, two microwavable pancakes, or cereal, depending on how I felt after my workout. Then at 9:00 a.m., I ate my morning snack, a small number of Cheez-its or pineapples or applesauce. I ate lunch around 11:00, which was before my three-hour mark, but this was the allotted time for the sixth-grade teachers to eat lunch. I cooked extra servings at dinner so I had leftovers to eat at lunchtime, so I had small portions of leftovers from dinner for lunch. On the nights I didn't have enough leftovers, I made a turkey and cheese, a ham and cheese, or a chicken salad sandwich.

I ate my afternoon snack of yogurt or applesauce around 2:45 or 3:00, which was also past the three-hour mark, but that was the only time I could fit it into my teaching schedule. This snack helped me withstand the temptation to eat the fattening snacks that were offered at staff and department meetings. I felt in control of my food choices, which was a good feeling. I ate dinner around 6:00, baking or grilling the selected meat for the night, and drastically cutting back on fried foods. It took a while for my husband to adjust to eating the healthier food, but he came around. The last meal allowed for the day was dessert, and it was optional. If I chose to eat dessert, I ate only a small portion.

The plan worked well, and I felt healthier and more energized. My exercise routine also helped me to lose a few pounds and maintain my ideal weight. Every once in a while, I went with Armecia to Balducci's for my Sante Fe chicken sandwich— whenever I decided to go out for lunch, she automatically knew where I wanted to go, and I even had Eric, the new math teacher, addicted to that sandwich—but when I became stressed, I didn't let food control me. I released my frustrations and relieved some stress during my workouts at the gym.

The gym on the base opened at 4:00 a.m., so that was when I woke up and began my gym routine. I lifted weights and ran at least a mile and a half, working out until 5:30 a.m. I was surprised at how many people were in the gym that time of morning. One morning I met a woman who told me that I should challenge myself and run a 5K. I thought there was no way I was going to participate in a 5K run, but I began to seriously think about making that a goal, and I started training to run the 3.2 miles. After training for a few months, I was ready for a 5K run. All I had to do was find one.

Middle school reform had made its way to Tilden, and our school was in phase one of the Middle School Reform movement. This meant we had extra staff-development training throughout the school year, and we had to return to school earlier than the other middle school teachers did. We also received Promethean boards in our classrooms so we had to learn the new technology. I liked the Promethean board because it was connected to the computer so it displayed my PowerPoint presentations. I no longer had to hook my laptop up the projector to show my PowerPoint presentations, but I was no longer able to write on my white board because the Promethean board covered it. If I wanted to write something on the new board, I had to use a special pen or type it on the computer. It was a mesmerizing board, but I had to adjust to it, and there was very little time to play with it before the first day of school because we were always in meetings or participating in staff-development activities. Once school started it was even harder for me to familiarize myself with the new technology because the curriculum became my focus. It took me almost the entire year to adapt to the Promethean board. The students would laugh at my attempts, but it was not in a mean way; it was more of a let-me-help-you-out-there, Mrs.-Wright way.

The sixth-grade team was the same as the year before, except for Eric, who replaced Emily as the math teacher. Jean, who was a seventh-grade English teacher, became the new sixth-grade English and reading teacher because Wendy moved upstairs to teach seventh-grade English and journalism. I was sad about not being able to see Wendy every day or to run across the hall to her room, but I felt a real connection with my team. We had team lunches, and we even went out to dinner later on in the year, which was a hilarious experience. I had learned their personalities, and they had learned mine: Len was laid back, easy-going, and funny, and he always told engaging stories about his children and his experiences. I knew I could talk to him when I had issues and that he would listen first and then give me solutions. He always told me what I needed to hear and not what I wanted to hear.

Mary Ellen and Laila knew almost everything about our teacher contract and other important county information. If I had a question about that stuff or anything else, they would help me. They were also good cooks, and they shared cooking tips with me. They joked that they would be my personal cooking instructors if I paid them the right price. Laila was laid back, and she always shared pictures of her grandchildren and told me funny stories. Mary Ellen was the type of person who would tell you how she really felt, but she was mostly like that strawberry candy that's hard on the outside and soft and sweet in the middle.

Kelly was quiet and friendly. We rarely saw each other during the school day, so one day she told me that we should get together for drinks after work, and we did. She was very reserved, but she talked if she was interested in the subject. Jean was very knowledgeable about books, plays, short stories, and just about anything that pertained to literature. (One day I hope I can be like her when it comes to literary knowledge.) Jean was also very thoughtful. One day at lunch, my team members were joking about the fact that I didn't eat bagels. Being a Southern girl, I preferred muffins and biscuits, but I love scones. One morning Jean walked into my class and handed me a small bag from Starbucks that contained a small scone. It was a perfect gift because I had not eaten breakfast that morning, and I hadn't had a scone in a while. She brightened my day with that scone.

If a topic bothered or interested Susie, she spoke her mind. Unlike me, she was very organized, so if I needed a copy of an assignment, I went to her room and she quickly found her copy.

Eric was different from anyone else on the team. Everyone on the team, except Mary Ellen and Len on a few occasions, was reserved for the most part, but Eric always spoke his mind and asked straightforward questions. He was like Ousier in *Steel Magnolias*, who walked right up to Annelle and asked her all sorts of personal questions while everyone nearby moved closer to hear her responses. That was Eric. He asked the questions you wanted to ask but would never ask yourself.

My teaching schedule was perfect. Because I was the coordinator for the after-school academic program, I taught only four classes—two English classes in the morning and two reading classes in the afternoon. This was going to be a great year! Well, not quite.

During one of the training sessions, we received a class list of our students and a list of students with Individual Education Plans (IEPs). I had almost thirty kids in every class except one. Not only were my class sizes huge, I had several students with IEPs in each class who needed special accommodations. It would not have been as big a deal if my class sizes had been smaller, but in my second-period class, four students needed a scribe, seven of them needed a read-aloud, and I had only one para-educator in the classroom. In third period, I had two para-educators— Rosa, the special education para-educator from second period, and Laurie—but the demand still exceeded the supply, as four students in this class needed a scribe, and five needed a read-aloud.

I remember once when all four of the students needed a scribe for the writing section of a test, and they had to wait their turn to go into the hall to dictate their answers so the other students couldn't hear them.

One of my students was prone to seizures, and I was nervous about that situation. He sometimes had seizures in the hallway, but then he started having them in his classes. I had a substitute the day he had a seizure in my class. After that day, Laurie casually positioned herself in his vicinity in case he had another one, as we did not want him to hurt himself. That was what worried me the most.

I felt overwhelmed throughout the entire school year, as I didn't know how I was going to meet the needs of all my students and ensure that all of them were successful. I not only had to worry about the accommodations, I also had to fill out an MCPS 272 form ("Secondary Teacher Report for Quarterly Progress") for each student each quarter and provide student work samples. I hated looking in my mailbox at the end of the quarter because I always had a thick folder filled with those 272 forms.

Since Kim was gone, Armecia became the person I used to keep my head on straight. I remember going to her room during my planning period on the first day of school, as we had the same period off. I walked into her room with my shoulders down and my head low. She was on the phone with her husband, but when she saw me, she told him that she would have to call him back.

I told her all about my third-period class, which was packed to the max. Some students had to sit at tables until I could get more desks. Along with a room full of students, I had two para-educators and the speech pathologist to assist me. I did not mind the speech pathologist being in my class, but I was distracted by her repeating everything I said. She tried to talk louder than I did, and she asserted herself as if she were the teacher. She also told me—rather than asking me—that she would be teaching some lessons during this period. I had a certain way of doing things, and I felt that she was trying to control my class. She was an older person and I respected her, and I thought it would be disrespectful to challenge her. I also told Armecia that I had huge inclusion classes and that, although almost all of the students with IEPs and 504 plans required priority seating, I didn't even have enough desks for all of the students. It was only the first day of school and I felt as if the weight of the world was on my shoulders.

Armecia told me that things would get better as the year progressed, and she warned me that I needed to make sure that I asserted myself so no one tried to take over my class. Thank God I didn't have to worry about the assertive part because later in the week the speech pathologist told me my curriculum was too rigid and she needed to be in a class with a more flexible curriculum. Armecia was also my e-mail-response filter. I did not have as many rude e-mails this year, but I did have a few, and I showed her my responses before I sent them to the parents. If something upset me, I went to Armecia's room, and she calmed me down.

One morning I opened my e-mail and a parent who had just checked Edline e-mailed me about her daughter's assignment that was two weeks late. Edline was an online system that allowed parents to track their children's grades and keep track of their progress in their classes. Whenever a teacher updated students' grades, the updates automatically appeared on Edline.

The grade for the assignment this parent was referring to had been posted for at least two weeks, so I told her that if her daughter turned in the assignment, I would give her half credit instead of a zero. I thought that was a generous offer, considering that the policy was that one day late equaled half credit, and an assignment turned in two days late did not have to be accepted at all. I guess she did not like that offer, because the next morning, Staci, the head of the special education department, approached me as I was putting my lunch in the refrigerator in the sixth-grade team room. She explained that the mother had e-mailed her and told her that her daughter had lost the assignment and had not asked for another one because she was afraid to. Staci said the student was going to ask me for another copy of the assignment and told me that I should give her full credit because she had an extended time accommodation.

Now, if the assignment had been two or three days late, I might have considered doing that, but this was two weeks late. The parent thought I was being unfair because her daughter had lost the assignment, but it had taken the parent two weeks to checked Edline and see the zero. I told Staci I was not going to give the student full credit and that she was lucky to get half credit. Staci was one of the nicest people you could ever meet, and I respected her, but I could not agree with her on this issue. She should have explained the extended time policy to the parent and agreed with me that half credit was more than fair. Eventually she agreed and told the parent that her daughter would have to receive half-credit. I wish she had sided with me from the beginning because many of the parents at Tilden have "Mommy-Daddy Syndrome"; that is, if they don't like what the teacher says, they go to the leader of a department or the principal to make the teacher change his or her decision. Even though I stuck to my guns during this incident, you have to choose your battles. Some disagreements are just not worth the time and effort.

For example, one parent demanded that the para-educator or I write sentence starters on her daughter's paper when I assigned questions that required written responses. I showed the student how to turn the question into a beginning sentence, but I could not hand-feed her everything. I taught the student how to think independently.

Some parents also thought that if their children had an IEP, they were supposed to pass the class automatically without doing any work. It was amazing how many parents wanted their children to have accommodations instead of asking how they could teach their children necessary life skills. For example, one student did not write neatly, so his mom wanted him tested so he could use the scribe accommodation. I concluded that all he needed to do was practice his writing technique, but the mom insisted that her son had a disability and demanded he be tested. (He was tested and he did not have a disability.) I believe that there are some kids who really do need accommodations, but the number of students who depend on accommodations is spiraling out of control.

Later in the year my class sizes decreased. During the fall and spring, the students take a MAP-R test that determines their reading level. Several of the students in my third-period class scored low on the test, so they were transferred out of my class and placed in a reading intervention program geared to struggling readers. The results from the MAP-R also changed the schedules of the students who scored high. One of my students scored high on the test, and even though she couldn't properly construct a sentence, she was moved to a GT class without anyone evaluating her work in the on-level class. I believed that the on-level curriculum was challenging enough for her, but the powers that be moved her without talking to me. Still, many of the students who transferred to the GT class after they scored high on the MAP-R went on to earn good grades.

As my class sizes decreased, the GT class sizes increased, and one teacher had more than thirty students in one class. The changes disturbed me because they were moving all of the students who scored high and keeping only the students who had C averages and below in the on-level classes. I believe that balance is important in the classroom because, if students see other students making As and Bs on assignments, then many students will strive to achieve that same success. However, if students see that their peers are making Cs, Ds, and Fs, they will feel as if they are doing fine as long as they get a C. My classes were already unbalanced because some of the students who belonged in the on-level class were enrolled in the GT class because many parents wanted their children to have the GT title or wanted their children in a challenging environment. In some cases, when the grades revealed that the GT curriculum was too challenging, they blamed the GT teacher instead of working with the teacher or moving their children into the proper course level. I was grateful when the administration stopped removing all the higher-performing students before they were all transferred to the GT class. By the end of the transfers, two of my classes were reduced to around twenty students, and in my IEP classes I had twenty-one students in second period and twenty-four in students in third period. Of course, this decrease in size did make these classes a little easier to manage!

One parent, who was a reading specialist at another school in the county, removed her son from my class because he had a C average and she thought that it was my fault. She e-mailed me with demands that I allow her son to redo almost every assignment and that I give him full credit for the many assignments he turned in late. Rather than giving in to her demands, I stuck to the county policy. The parent went to the principal and demanded that her son be moved to a GT class, and within a week he was moved. I went to Jennifer and asked her why this parent was allowed to do this, and she told me that it was the parent's option and there was nothing that could be done.

I knew and the parent knew her child would not be able to keep pace with the GT class, and that we were setting him up for failure. Then the student began to brag to the other students in the class that he was moving to a GT class, and the students who had earned As and Bs told me that it was unfair to move this C student to the GT class. I could not tell them that I had nothing to do with the schedule change, but I understood their confusion. His mother put him back in an on-level class the next school year.

As the year progressed, I began to feel sad and depressed and to experience severe headaches on the left side of my head, like someone was hammering a nail into my head. The pain did not go away with aspirin, and I began to have mini seizure-like jerks. While they lasted only a few seconds, during these seconds I could not speak. Then the lymph nodes in my neck swelled up like ping-pong balls.

Coordinating the after school program probably contributed to some of the stress because I had to make sure there were enough kids enrolled in the program or the classes would be canceled and there would be no program. Then I had to make sure I had enough teachers and materials for each class and collect data on student progress in the program. There were also times when I had to manage student behavior and call parents because their children refused to attend the program.

My symptoms started before Christmas break and faded away by the end of January. My dad told me that stress was causing my body to react this way, but I thought that if it were stress, the symptoms would go away during Christmas break. Eventually I went to see my doctor and I was given three different types of pills to control the pain, relax my muscles, and help me sleep. I was also given an MRI since this was the first time I had ever experienced the jerks.

I soon realized that I was under a lot of self-inflicted pressure to be the perfect teacher, as I did not want anyone in my class to fail. It hit me hard when the majority of my students had low C or D averages; I wanted my students to be successful. However, more students than usual were not motivated and didn't care that they were failing their classes. At one of our team meetings, we agreed that this particular group of sixth-grade students was more interested in the social aspect of school than the academic aspect. They talked more about Facebook, cell phones, and who was having a party that weekend than they did about homework, tests, and anything related to school.

What's more, most of the parents of these students were not actively involved in their children's education. A few parents were mad at me because they felt that their children had been assigned accommodations, so they should automatically be passing my class. I went over concepts with the students, and they would practice, both independently and cooperatively. Then we reviewed the practice assignment. However, when I graded the formative or summative assessment I was disappointed. What was even more disappointing was that everyone did well during the practice but then scored poorly on the test. I thought I was doing something wrong. I retaught and reviewed, but only a few of the students showed improvement. I tutored a few students who stayed after school and still saw little improvement. Were my expectations too high? The students commented that they loved my class, and the parents reported that their children enjoyed my class, but only a few students made significant improvement from the first quarter to the fourth quarter.

Some students became more involved by the fourth quarter, and I tried to use that to lessen my disappointment, but I had only a few As and Bs that year. Students usually adjusted to the class routines by second quarter, but not this particular school year; I was still reinforcing classroom procedures and expectations in the middle of the fourth quarter. I realized that if a student was not motivated and determined to do better, then it did not matter what strategies I used to reteach and review; I would still see no results.

Since so many sixth-graders were performing poorly in many of their classes, the assistant principal had a conference with them, something I had never seen him do before. He told all of them to go to their teachers and ask for any make-up or missing work, but only some did. Lack of student motivation was a school-wide problem that had increased significantly compared to my first year at Tilden.

One day in April I opened my school e-mail and discovered a message about the Susan G. Komen Global Race for the Cure in Washington, DC, on Saturday, June 6. Jane, one of my colleagues, had formed a team entitled Lenore's Legacy in remembrance of her sister. I loved Jane, and her sarcasm was hilarious; she reminded me of Chandler Bing from *Friends*. I registered for the race.

I remember race day like it was yesterday. It was a perfect day because it was overcast and there was a nice breeze. I took the Green Line to the Yellow Line and arrived at the Archives-Navy

Memorial-Penn Quarter station. Then I walked to the Newseum, where we had all agreed to gather at 7:30 a.m. I arrived earlier than I thought I would, so I walked to the sponsors' tents and looked at their displays. There were a great number of people. After browsing for few minutes, I went back to the Newseum and met with my team. I spoke with Jane and the other members of the team, and Mary Ellen attached my race number to the back of my shirt. Then I headed toward the starting line. I was the only member of our team who would be running; everyone else was walking. After a long opening ceremony, the race started. I was pumped and ready to run.

The walkers walked the same course we ran, so as I was running back toward the finish line, the walkers were on the other side. I occasionally glanced over at the walkers to see if I could spot any of my teammates, but I never did. The next thing I knew, the huge "Finish Line" sign loomed ahead, a huge timer below it. My finishing time was thirty-six minutes.

After the race/walk we all met at Jane's car for snacks, and after enjoying some fellowship for about thirty minutes, we went our separate ways. I caught the Green Line at the Gallery Place Metro station and went home. I had initially dismissed the idea of running a 5K, but now I had accomplished a goal and it was gratifying.

The year seemed to drag on forever, but June 16, 2009, finally arrived. We walked with the students to the bus and waved goodbye. As I was walking back to my classroom, I realized that I had just completed my fifth year of teaching. I had survived the first five years of my teaching career.

Chapter Seven

Reflection on the First Five Years

During my fifth year of teaching, I became
discouraged by the lack of student interest and
motivation, and I realized that a successful student
relies not only on himself or herself and the work
of the teacher, but also on positive parental involvement. In
college, I researched and wrote papers on the topic of parental
involvement, but researching it was not the same as experiencing
it. I have encountered many kinds of parents and never imagined
that any parent would treat me the way some of them did. I was
not prepared for the disrespect and the feeling of inferiority. I
have grouped the types of parents that I have encountered into
four categories: uninvolved, blame the teacher, on top of things,
and pushy.

The "uninvolved" parent allows his or her child to fail. When
interims and report cards are sent home, he or she does not contact
the school to arrange a parent-teacher conference to determine how
the child could be more successful in school. I tried to contact this
type of parent through e-mail and phone calls to set up a parent
conference in response to their children's low achievement, but
they never took the initiative to call back. They never seemed to
have the time, or they made appointments but cancelled them
at the last minute. It is hard for some students with this type of
parent to be successful in school because there is no one at home
making sure their homework is done or checking their grades to
see if classwork is being completed.

I learned to continue to reach out to these parents and inform
them of their children's progress (or lack of progress) through
e-mails and phone calls. I also continued to encourage the children
of these parents to turn in homework and complete assignments as
much as possible, even though I knew their nonchalant attitude

was due to the lack of parental support at home. During my second year at Tilden, I had a student who had the potential to perform better on his assignments, but he told me that his mom didn't care, so he didn't care. It was disheartening to see such a waste of talent. I believe that, had his mom shown concern, his attitude would have changed.

The "blame the teacher" parent waits until the end of the semester to look at his or her child's grades. Even though they have had access to their children's grades and interim reports throughout the semester, they proclaim that it is the teachers' fault that their children are failing.

One year at Tilden, I had a student who was on a behavior contract. The sixth-grade team had a parent conference with the student's mother the first nine weeks, but when we tried to contact her during the second nine weeks to set up another team conference, she did not respond. We met as a team, without the mother, to devise strategies, but it was as if she had given up on her son and had accepted that he was going to misbehave in school. The last week of the second nine weeks, she e-mailed all of her son's teachers and told us that it was our fault that her son was not doing his homework because the work that we sent home was too difficult. She claimed that no one had contacted her about his grades, and that we had just sat back and let her son fail our classes. She knew her child was not doing his work in class or at home and that he was misbehaving in school, but she did not work with the teachers to solve the problem. It was easier to blame the teachers.

I learned that documentation is very important when dealing with this type of parent. I kept a binder with a list of the days and times I called these parents and the copies of the e-mails I sent them. I learned that I had to be patient and not to take what these parents said personally because their anger was misplaced. These parents knew their children were not performing to their level of ability, and they felt helpless and frustrated.

The "on top of things" parent is the involved parent. These parents are involved with their children and their children's teachers. If their children are struggling in a subject, they tell them to seek the teacher's help. If their children bring home low grades, they e-mail or call the teacher to set up a conference to see what their children are doing wrong, and they work with the teacher to find resolutions to the problem. There is no accusing but plenty of discussion about what needs to be done by all parties to achieve success. These parents do not harass the teacher but teach their children to advocate for themselves. These parents make sure their children are studying for tests and doing their homework. There is a healthy parent-teacher relationship that benefits the student, teacher, and parent alike.

The "pushy" parent tries to bully the teacher to get his or her way. These parents meet with the principal and threaten to meet with the superintendent if they disagree with a teacher's professional decision, even if the decision is aligned with the district's policies.

Here's an example: I used to give my students their vocabulary words at least a week in advance so they would have enough time to study them. One of my students was absent the day before the vocabulary quiz and thought she would be exempt from taking the quiz the day it was given, but I reminded her that she knew what day the quiz was and that she had had plenty of time to study for it. Her mother called me and said I was treating her daughter unfairly. Then she sent an e-mail to the principal and me, demanding a conference. During the conference she told me that none of my students studied for my vocabulary tests in advance; they all waited until the night before to study. I told her that that was their choice, but they were responsible for being prepared. Then the mother began to call me names and insisted that this was a conspiracy against her daughter. She told the superintendent that the school and I had it out for her daughter because she was African American.

Later, she sent me an e-mail that stated, "I have called and left messages for all of you, the principal, guidance counselor, and Ms. Wright. You will not make my daughter's last year at this school miserable to the point that she cannot learn! Ms. Wright, you seem hell bent on using your grade book to punish her because of our conference. Please believe me I will not rest until she is out of your class! Me and my husband will be at the school at today at 1:00 p.m."

Her bullying did not stop there. She sent me another e-mail that stated, "I know I will not have to work nearly as hard to get her away from the likes of an overanxious rookie wanna be teacher trying to prove herself by playing hardball with a child as you have been in your efforts to fail my child. Please grow up and deal with parents showing concern, parent to parent and stop hiding behind your grade book and using your so called authority to get at me through my daughter! How sad that you call yourself a teacher! You are nothing more than a TOKEN."

She was the perfect example of a pushy parent. Her daughter was removed from my class to prevent any further abusive e-mails or interactions with the parent, but she continued to send abusive messages. This parent became so aggressive that she was eventually prohibited from contacting me and threatened with a restraining order if she did. The most disturbing thing about this situation was that it started simply because her daughter did not study for a vocabulary test.

The pushy parent is often rude and vicious. I learned that responding the way I wanted to respond did not help the situation but only made it worse. I learned never to have a one-on-one conference with this type of parent but always to include the principal or assistant principal. When I contacted the parent, I forwarded a copy of the e-mail to the principal. I kept a record of my conversations and interactions with the parent in a file folder for documentation. Documentation is the most important part of dealing with this type of parent.

I believe that change is good for staving off complacency and the tendency to go through the motions. Being a military wife has provided me the opportunity to experience two different school settings. I have experienced difficult school environments, where some students came to school hungry and had only two sets of clothing that had to be alternated throughout the week, where I had a room full of students whose main goal was to get me to pack my bags and leave the class, where intervention programs had to be implemented constantly in order to have any chance of running the class, where behavior problems prevented me from teaching because I had to spend half of the period dealing with student behavior instead of focusing on the curriculum. I have also experienced a teaching environment where most of the students don't have to worry about money, where students come into the class quietly and ready to learn. I have learned a lot from both experiences, and they have helped shape me as a professional.

The past five years of teaching have taught me important lessons about how to survive in this profession. I learned that it is important to form confident relationships with other teachers and that working with the other teachers in my discipline is beneficial. I realized that it is okay to make mistakes, but I have to make sure that I am open-minded to advice on how to correct them. I learned that I should always be open to others' ideas, even if I don't plan to use them. I learned how to talk about what is bothering me and how to share my frustrations and disappointments and to be open to solutions to the problems I face. I learned not to hold stuff inside because it will only build up until one day everything explodes. I learned that it's important to have teacher friends who will tell you what you need to hear and not what you want to hear. I learned that the administration is important to the success of the school and that if the administration does not support the teachers, the students will not respect the teachers. I learned that student motivation and parent involvement are necessary for student achievement and success in the classroom and that everyone—the teacher, the student, the parents, and the administration—have to work together if a student is to be successful in the classroom. However, if one link is missing, teaching and learning can become very difficult and disheartening.

Most important, I learned that I love teaching and that teaching is a tough job. There will always be ups and downs, but in the end, it's worth the journey!